THE CONTAGIOUS CONGREGATION

THE CONTAGIOUS CONGREGATION

Frontiers in Evangelism and Church Growth

George G. Hunter III

ABINGDON PRESS   NASHVILLE

THE CONTAGIOUS CONGREGATION

Copyright © 1979 by Abingdon

Eighth Printing 1984

Library of Congress Cataloging in Publication Data

HUNTER, GEORGE G.
   The contagious congregation.
   Bibliography: p.
   1. Evangelistic work. 2. Church growth. I. Title.
BV3790.H89   254´.5   78-12322

ISBN 0-687-09490-9

MANUFACTURED BY THE PARTHENON PRESS AT
NASHVILLE, TENNESSEE, UNITED STATES OF AMERICA

I dedicate this book,
with deep affection and appreciation, to

DONALD SOPER
and
DONALD McGAVRAN

pioneers of twenty-first–century evangelism

Soper's lifetime discoveries in London's open-air
forums, about preevangelizing resistant people and
McGavran's lifetime discoveries about finding and
evangelizing receptive people will be among the
cornerstones of informed evangelization in the next
generation.

ACKNOWLEDGMENTS

Whatever muscle and nourishment may be found in this book results from the author having grazed in more green pastures than Man-O'-War. For many years I have sponged the thoughts and models of selected pioneers and practitioners in Christian evangelism, reflected, and, in rare instances, improved on them. Some future punster will be more right than he knows when he suggests that "all work and no plagiarism makes Hunter a dull pedagogue." I would now like to express deep gratitude to a number of persons.

I acknowledge and celebrate the influences of some early significant others; Orville Nelson, under whom I answered the call to enter the ministry; and several college, seminary, and graduate school professors—particularly Henry Barnett, Ted Runyon, William R. Cannon, Mack B. Stokes, Norman Perrin, John Jellicorse, and Franklyn Haiman.

My years with the old Methodist Board of Evangelism were formative. Lawrence Lacour raised and faced many of the questions and issues that several of us have been dealing with ever since. Ed Beck, Joe Hale, George Morris, George Fallon, Kermit Long, Tex Evans, Roberto Escamilla and Harold Bales contributed more than they know as colleagues.

I first ventilated some of this material to my classes during several years of teaching in the McCreless Chair of Evangelism at the Perkins School of Theology, Southern Methodist University. I thank my many students for what I learned from them, and Joseph Quillian, Jim Ward, Leroy Howe, Howard Grimes, and Richey Hogg for much support and encouragement.

This book represents a ministry by my family to the larger community. My wife, Ella Fay, is a contagious example of what the kind of evangelism taught in this book can achieve. My children, Gill and Monica, were patient enough to defer some playtime while Daddy hacked away at an "umpteenth draft." My parents, George and Barbara Hunter very early planted some of the dreams that are behind this project—and some of the last rethinking and rewriting was done in my Dad's bedroom just a few days after his unexpected death.

I especially thank several men who modeled evangelism possibilities for me at the very times when I deeply needed a look at authentic possibilities, notably, E. Stanley Jones, Harry Denman, Bryan Green, and Alan Walker. More recently, I have been influenced by J. Wascom Pickett, Peter Wagner, Alan Tippett, Arthur Glasser, Win Arn, Ezra Earl Jones, Wendell Belew, Kenneth Chafin, and Lyle Schaller. It may have been one of Lloyd Ogilvie's sermons at First Presbyterian Church, Hollywood that first suggested this book's title to me.

My friend and secretarial colleague, Mrs. Jo Hicks, used her typewriter to add her order to my ardor, and

whatever literary qualities this book possesses stem from
her subtle suggestions—such as, "this sentence makes
no sense."

I conclude by acknowledging my deep indebtedness
to the two men whose careers, thoughts, writings, and
counsels are most obviously reflected in these writings—
and to whom I dedicate this book: Dr. Donald Lord
Soper of the West London Methodist Mission and Dean
Donald McGavran of Fuller Seminary's School of World
Mission.

CONTENTS

FOREWORD... **15**

I CAN OUR CONGREGATIONS BECOME
   CONTAGIOUS?................................... **19**
   But, What Is Evangelism?...................... 21
   Concrete Working Definitions................ 25

II A NEW MODEL FOR CHRISTIAN
   WITNESSING.................................... **35**
   The Deductive Model of Christian Witnessing...... 38
   Begin with Human Motives................... 39
   A Philosophy for Appealing to Motives............ 40
   Maslow's Hierarchy of Human Motives............. 41
   How to Use Maslow's Hierarchy in Evangelism... 43
   The Inductive Model of Christian Witnessing....... 45
   The Inductive-Grace Model................... 47
   The Inductive-Mission Model................. 48
   How to Begin with People.................... 51
   Beginning at the Middle..................... 53
   Qualifying the Inductive Model.............. 54
   The Inductive Model Commended............ 57

Postscript: What About Counseling
    Seekers into Faith? 60

III A PROVEN MODEL FOR
    COMMUNICATING THE GOSPEL **64**
    The Message 66
    The Audience 70
    The Communicator 76

IV COMMUNICATING THE GOSPEL TO
    RESISTANT SECULAR PEOPLE **80**
    The Basic Fact of our Secular Age 83
    Generalizations About Secular People 86
    From Knowledge to Ignorance 91
    From Death to Life 92
    From Guilt to Doubt 93
    From Need to Curiosity 95
    From Belonging to Alienation 96
    Strategies for Communicating the Gospel
       to Resistant Secular People 97
    Relevant Facets of the Message 101

V THE GRAND STRATEGY: DISCOVER
    RECEPTIVE PEOPLE **104**
    A New Motivation for Urgency 106
    Indigenous Methods for Receptive
       People 108
    The Policy for Resistant People 111
    Introducing Indicators 112
    General Indicators 113
    Third World Indicators 115
    Guidelines for Discovering Receptive
       Mainline Americans 117
    A Suggestion for Strategy 128

VI THE LOCAL CONGREGATION PUTS
    IT TOGETHER **130**
    "Wait to Receive Power" 131

"Go into Your World" 134

"Preach the Gospel—Be My
  Witnesses" 137

"Baptize Them into the Church and
  Teach Them" 143

The Contagious Congregation's Mission Beyond
  the Parish 145

NOTES **153**

FOREWORD

Here is a rich book couched in pungent English. It talks good sense, makes needed distinctions clearly, and disagrees with erroneous positions courteously. It is good reading.

This book addresses itself to Problem Number One in mainline denominations and congregations all across America, and indeed, around the world. If the church is to continue to "do justly and love kindness," it must at least continue to exist. Really, it ought to grow in size and effectiveness. Instead of which, many churches have been declining. The famous "First Church" in many a city had twenty-four hundred members and now has only eleven hundred. Though it has excellent music, great preaching, cushioned pews, and a friendly manner, it grows smaller, decade by decade. Getting such typical congregations and denominations growing again is a most urgent task. George Hunter speaks powerfully to it.

He speaks effectively in contemporary language—vivid, colorful, and readable. He is a modern. This book will be read by ministers of all denominations with profit.

Lay leaders also will enjoy it and move to more effective service.

Dr. Hunter assumes that the conviction required for "making disciples" is already there—needing only to be aroused, harnessed, and put to work. I hope he is right. Any *lasting* passion for evangelism rises only out of rock-ribbed convictions. Churches which have lost these convictions don't grow. Oh, they may put on some bright new program and get a quick surge of growth, bringing in a few dozen or a few hundred, but ten years later they are smaller than ever. Something much more final than a value system built on consensus is required to fuel lasting reproductivity. Becoming a Christian must be seen as and believed to be a passing from darkness to light, from death to life—not the joining of a rather pleasant religious club.

The most effective use of this book will be as a study manual. Let a group of earnest Christians give each member a copy, read a chapter a week, and meet to discuss it. Let them ask two questions: (1) What does it say? (2) What does it mean for this congregation?

This book can readily be put into action, clothed in deeds, buttressed by new allocations of men and money, directed toward new high ends, and bathed in prayer. John Wesley would have rejoiced in it. Dr. Hunter has given us tools for the task. Let us use them.

Donald McGavran
Fuller Theological Seminary

THE CONTAGIOUS
CONGREGATIONS

CHAPTER I

CAN OUR CONGREGATIONS BECOME CONTAGIOUS?

I believe that mainline Protestant Christianity, although declining today, can and will once again become a contagious movement among the peoples of North America. The essential ingredients for such a resurgence are already present: We now *know* more about how effective evangelization takes place than any other generation has ever known. Greater numbers of people are receptive to The Faith than have been in quite some time. And great numbers of congregations are perceiving that the rusty swords evangelizers used in the past will be impotent tomorrow in the serious battle for the attention and devotion of the many people bent on worshiping and following something.

Such congregations, by the thousands, are openly searching for new handles to better grasp the Great Commission mandate, "Go . . . and make disciples." For instance, as I write this I see on my desk an urgent letter from a United Methodist Council director. Writing of a metropolitan congregation in New York City, he explains:

The church has a two-minister staff, both highly capable men. The building is new and attractive. The preaching is good. The music is excellent. The worship is flexible and exciting. Yet, the church does not grow. What kinds of intervention might work in a situation like this?

That is the question thousands of congregations are asking. "We have strength and much going for us. Why do so many people ignore what we have to offer?"

Perhaps one reason this metropolitan congregation is not growing is that it does not really offer what it has to offer! If it did, it would make a difference. Lyle Schaller, from his twenty years of research into congregations, reports that one characteristic that nearly every growing congregation has in common is "an active evangelistic emphasis" which "has its most important expression in lay persons."[1] Notice that in this nongrowing congregation, there is no mention of such an emphasis outreach and the lack of growth is not coincidental. Most people in a community never know what a congregation has to offer or that it wants to share it, unless people from the congregation leave the church and enter the neighborhood to engage others in caring friendship and meaningful conversation and so open up the faith and life of the congregation as a live option to undiscipled people.

This is one reason why so many congregations do not grow—they do not engage in intentional "evangelism." The other reason is that they *do* engage in evangelism—but in ways which are outmoded, or not "indigenous" to the culture of the target population. So, some churches fail to grow because they do not evangelize, others because they do—but in ineffective forms. And, in many cases, the forms which an "evangelistic" congregation uses turn off the other congregation and make it harder rather than easier to encourage them to evangelize.

This book desires to inspire and equip the leaders of congregations to evangelize in ways that with integrity really do attract people, that make new disciples, that expand Christ's church, and that make evangelism a credible word and enterprise again.

BUT, WHAT IS EVANGELISM?

The ministry by which a congregation shares The Faith, makes new disciples, and thereby becomes contagious is called "evangelism," or sometimes "evangelization." Evangelism is a much misunderstood word, capable of many possible meanings. Most people swear either by it or at it. An adequate understanding of what evangelism is and purposes is indispensable to a congregation's achievement of contagion. It is not enough to suggest that evangelism is the offering to people of what we have to offer. By way of preview, I will conclude by suggesting that whatever else one might mean by evangelism, one must necessarily mean the "making of new Christian disciples."

In America, various types of ministry are called evangelism. I have found it possible (with some oversimplifying) to categorize such ministries under five headings based on their basic rhetorical appeal to people, including the response they are asking for, and on what they "report" to their board or constituency. Please note, all of the five ministries at their best are valid, are rooted in scripture, and help people. But, in the considered judgment of the worldwide Church Growth movement, only one merits the term evangelism in its classical, apostolic, Great Commission sense.

The first type of ministry, frequently called evangelism, basically says to people "LET US HELP YOU." This is the ministry of loving Christian presence. This ministry purposes to be present with people, identify with them, serve them, share in their struggles, work to liberate them from injustice, etc. The world-renowned practitioner of this splendid approach to ministry is Mother Theresa of Calcutta, but there are many more. The writer who most identifies this type of ministry with "evangelism" is Colin Williams.[2] If you were to write Mother Theresa and ask for a report of last year's work, they would report how many dying people, etc. they had *helped* in their ministry.

Second, whereas some practitioners are appealing to people to "Let Us Help You," others are saying "LET GOD HELP YOU." This ministry is usually called evangelism, and its practitioners are called evangelists. American practitioners of this vintage such as the late Kathryn Kuhlman, Oral Roberts, and Robert Schuller come to mind as illustrations. They distinctly vary from each other, and much of what they do for people spills out of this neat category, but they are all attempting to persuade people to let God intervene in their lives to help them in some way—to heal them, give them self-confidence, confer some gift upon them, or bless them. In their reports, they celebrate how many people wrote in testifying to God's intervening help. Such ministries are also biblically valid, but they do not have as their central and indispensible objective the making of new Christian disciples. So, while they are legitimate and necessarily involve persuading people to receive God's ministry to them, they should not be thought of as evangelism in the New Testament sense. People can receive our help and/or God's help without becoming *followers* of Jesus Christ. I commend the New Testament case of the ten lepers as Exhibit A.

Third, many Christians, in another approach to ministry also called evangelism, are saying "HEAR THE WORD!" They believe that evangelism is virtually synonymous with proclamation, telling the good news, getting the Story out. Proclaiming becomes an end in itself, and although one may hope for the hearer's response and commitment, one is evangelizing simply by getting the word out—whether people accept it or not. This (mis)understanding is fairly dominant with some British writers, such as J. I. Packer and John Strott. It is also the assumption transparent in much of radio and television ministry. Radio evangelists typically report how many stations they are on or the size of the listening audience to indicate how many people are hearing the Word.

Fourth, many approaches to persuasion-ministry basically appeal to people to "MAKE A DECISION." The objective of this type of ministry is to elicit from people at a recordable and memorable point in time an act of the will called a *decision*. This is the salient objective of virtually all "crusade evangelism"—all the way from the mass crusades of Billy Graham to the one-to-one crusade evangelism of Campus Crusade. To their constituencies, such evangelists report how many decisions were obtained in a particular target audience or period of time.

Fifth, another approach to ministry that is also called evangelism (and is the one I am commending) appeals to people to "BECOME CHRISTIAN DISCIPLES." This evangelism has two related objectives for people: (1) that they become *lifetime followers* of Jesus Christ as their Lord, living by his power and his will, in their lives, relationships, and world, and (2) that they be *incorporated into Christ's Body*—the church or messianic community.

This approach to evangelizing is mandated in the Great Commission (Matt. 28:19-20) and is dramatized throughout the Acts of the Apostles. The early church went about "making disciples" who were soon found in Christ's church devoted "to the apostles' teaching and fellowship, to the breaking of bread and the prayers" (Acts 2:42). In this approach, the messianic community, as in Acts, reports how many *disciples* are responsibly involved in the church.

This essential approach was rediscovered by John Wesley, who throughout his public career appealed to people to give their lives to Jesus Christ as his followers and submit to the rigors, the support, and the enabling power of an indigenous form of the church—the class meeting. This Great Commission, disciple-making approach is at the heart of the worldwide Church Growth movement in this generation. I believe that the mainline Protestant denominations are evolving toward this conscious, new disciple-making stance, and that if this trend continues, soon our own people will no longer need to feel that the approach of parachurch organizations is "more biblical" than that of the churches!

None of what I have said should be interpreted as a denouncement of the other four approaches to ministry. At their best, they are rooted in scripture and achieve much for people. Furthermore, the objectives of the other four approaches are often definite stages in the prediscipling of many people. That is, we are not likely to make new Christian disciples unless: (1) we achieve a loving presence among them, (2) they discover the Spirit of God intersecting their lives or approaching them, (3) they hear the gospel, and (4) they make important decisions for the new life in Christ. But whenever any of these objectives are regarded as ends in themselves rather than as means toward the apostolic goal of making new disciples, then such ministries—however intrinsically valid—should never be considered as evangelism. Indeed, those ministries engaged in as ends in themselves may unwittingly militate against the making of real disciples. The partial dose may innoculate against the full possibility. Witness how many people in our culture have heard the Word and believe in its truth, but are not actual followers of Christ through any local congregation. Witness how many persons once made a decision for Christ, but today are not involved in any believing community nor seek Christ's will and power for their lives.

So, evangelism is the church intentionally offering what it supremely has to offer—the opportunity to follow Jesus Christ within the life, fellowship, and ministries of a congregation. Whatever else one may legitimately believe evangelism to include, this is its indispensible focus. I believe that disciple-making is at the very heart of the emerging Protestant consensus on the meaning of evangelism and that it will become the dominant understanding in the 1980s.

CONCRETE WORKING DEFINITIONS

Let's shift gears because I have not yet defined evangelism concretely enough for most Christians to really grasp the idea and begin planned intentional evangelizing on the basis of it. Evangelism can also be defined in terms of *its participants*. That is, disciple-making evangelism is a ministry of reaching out that *we, Christ,* and the *receiver* are jointly engaged in. What follows are three extensively field-tested definitions—enough to let the would-be evangelizing congregation know where to hedge its bets and have a clear self-identity and purpose in outreach.

Definition One: Evangelism is what *WE* do to help make the Christian faith, life, and mission a live option to undiscipled people, both outside and inside the congregation.

A. *Disciple-making evangelism necessarily involves* US, *members of the believing Body of Christ.* "Christ has no hands but our hands, . . . no feet but our feet, . . . no tongues but our tongues, . . . " Although he creates receptivity in people by his prevenient grace, he must make his appeal through us, his ambassadors (II Cor. 5:20). So evangelism is not a work that we can merely leave up to God. It doesn't get done without *evangelizers'* reaching out in ways that are appropriate to a target population.

B. *Our objective is to help bring people into the full Christian faith, life, and mission*—so that they might fulfill God's will, become the persons they were born to be, and participate in Christ's total mission. Expressed in negative terms, the objective of disciple-making evangelism is *not* merely to save souls or get decisions. It is to make new Christian disciples.

C. *Our role is to make this new life based on following Christ a live option for all human beings.* It is not our task to manipulate or jockey or psych or maneuver or in any way coerce human beings into coming forward or signing on the dotted line or joining our churches to pad our membership statistics. It is our calling to work jointly with Christ's Spirit in making Faith a live option. We are called to place and keep this option for life in the forefront of their consciousness and to model and interpret it clearly and relevantly, so that the option of following Jesus is always an inescapable possibility in their consciousness. We also exist to probe them at points in time that seem to be "God's moment," in which they may be especially receptive, to see whether they are ready to consciously commit their life and future to Christ and his church, and to seek social support for growing in that commitment.

D. *The target population for Christian evangelism is undiscipled people* i.e., people who are not yet followers of Jesus Christ through his special family, the church. Our objectives are twofold: (1) that they become followers of Jesus Christ (2) that they be incorporated into the life of Christ's church. This actually means that *part* of our mission is to church members for whom the second objective has been achieved to some degree, but who are not yet committed followers of Jesus. But we must not overstress this undiscipled population that is already within the Church. There are two dangerous myths regarding church members. One myth is that we neglect them and spend too much time reaching out to total outsiders; but, in fact, more than 90 percent of all our evangelism programs and our evangelizing time is targeted toward nominal church members. The other myth is that we must win our own nominal Christians and inactive members *before* we can evangelize outsiders, but frequently our own immunized nominals and inactives are more resistant to the challenge to discipleship than are rank pagans! There are approximately 155 million undiscipled persons in America today in whom both of the above objectives have not been achieved. As I shall elaborate later, our primary calling is to reach out to those who are receptive—while they are receptive. In surveying our local mission field, we are not especially interested in whether people say they "believe in the existence of a Supreme Being" or express a church preference. We follow the undiluted criterion of the first-century apostolic church: Are you (or are you not) a follower of Jesus the Messiah through the messianic community?

Definition Two: Evangelism is also what JESUS CHRIST does through the church's *kerygma* (message), *koinonia* (fellowship), and *diakonia* (service) to set people free.

A. *The Christian mission to find and disciple lost people is originally and primarily Christ's mission.* By his invitation we participate in his mission. He desires to employ us and make his appeal through our presence and witness. He initiates his mission to people by means of his prevenient grace, i.e., the Spirit moving through the events and circumstances of their lives to create receptivity and make possible a faith-response to the great news. So when faith, through our friendship and witness, begins to awaken in a person's being, this is not supremely due to us but to the Spirit's work within them.

B. *Christ works in the ministry of evangelism to set people free.* He wants to free them from the sins, fears, hangups, oppressions, demons, and tyrannies that prevent and frustrate their becoming the people they were born to be and deeply within themselves have always wanted to be. Christ wants to free them for faith, hope, love, justice, reconciliation, peace-making, and self-fulfillment in him.

C. *Christ does his evangelistic work through the church's kerygma, koinonia,* and *diakonia.* All three of these resources of our multi-faceted gospel are basic to the evangelization of persons.

That the proclamation or sharing of the kergyma (the Christian message or "great news") is basic to evangelism should come as no surprise. Jesus, the apostles, and the early church were all conspicuous in their proclamation of the gospel. Paul declared that "it pleased God through the folly of what we preach to save those who believe" (I Cor. 1:21). Whatever passes for evangelism today is usually so labeled because the preaching is the central activity (although some of America's most conspicuous preaching today teaches more about America's civil religion than the apostolic gospel). Sharing the content of the gospel is indispensible to evangelizing in any age, for by its story people are informed of and taught a new possibility for life. So God uses our proclaiming or teaching sacramentally to speak his living Word to receptive people and so awaken a faith-response to his grace.

Koinonia is not widely perceived to be basic to evangelizing, but it is as intrinsic and indispensible as kerygma. Koinonia is the setting in which the contagion of the Christian possibility is communicated. As Lord Soper exclaims, "If it is from Kerygma that the Christian faith is taught, it is within Koinonia that the Christian faith is caught." Kenneth Scott Latourette, in the first volume of his *History of the Expansion of Christianity,* contends that the early church probably attracted as many people to the faith through the inclusiveness, support, and power of its contagious fellowship as it did through its preaching. Today, the contagious congregation will also be conscious of the attracting power of a believing, loving fellowship. It will work to make and keep its groups and classes open, affirming, and welcoming toward new-comers. It will continually create many more new groups and classes—who will also form a relevant agenda for seeking outsiders.

Diakonia (Christian service, both in its one-to-one helping expression and its social reform expression) is also basic to effective evangelism—for two reasons. First, a serving church provides credibility for the message it announces and the fellowship which people are being invited to join. For example, the message of reconcilia-tion, new life, justice, peace, love for others is much more likely to be believed when it is announced by a congregation whose members are in fact observed to be reconciled, serving the needy, making peace, etc. Second, until seekers themselves begin following Jesus Christ in loving, serving ministry, the discipleship option remains only a possibility—believed perhaps, its attrac-tion felt perhaps, but not yet incarnated in a new Christian personality. If it is by kerygma that the Christian faith is taught, and by koinonia that it is caught, then it is as a by-product of diakonia that the Christian faith is bought! In its evangelism, the contagious congregation will invite people to join Christ and his people in actual projects and serving ministries, and the congregation will structure varied ministry opportunities for all of its people.

Definition Three: Evangelizing happens when the *RECEIVER* (receptor, respondent) turns (1) to Christ, (2) to the Christian message and ethic, (3) to a Christian congregation, and (4) to the world, in love and mission—*in any order.*

This definition stresses *where* the receiver consciously plugs in to appropriate the Christian possibility and realize it in his own life. The four turnings above represent a merger of the models of two missionary scholars. D. T. Niles, in *That They May Have Life,*[4] contended that three turnings must take place in the prospective Christian's life: (1) to Christ, (2) to Christian ideas and ideals, and (3) to some form of Christian congregation. Niles mentions that these turnings generally take place one at a time in a person's life and in any conceivable order. Bishop Stephen Neill, in a conversation with the present writer, said that for the last twenty years he has had three conscious objectives for people in his own evangelism: that they turn (1) to Jesus Christ, (2) to some Church, and (3) "to a vision of and a passion for a Christian world"—that would emerge both from evangelization and justice. He added, "By the way, these turnings generally take place one at a time, and can take place in any conceivable order." Modifying some of these terms I have merged the models of Niles and Neill into a four-point model.

The church's RESOURCES through which Christ works	The RECEIVER'S TURNINGS which appropriate Christ's work
	to Christ
Kerygma (message) ←——→	to Christian message and ethic
Koinonia (fellowship) ←——→	to a Christian congregation
Diakonia (service) ←——→	to the world, in love and mission

It will be readily perceived that the last three of the *turnings* closely parallel the three *resources* through which Christ works (see Definition Two, C). These parallels are not accidental. Each of the two columns represents the same reality but from a different vantage point—the left, from the church's perspective, the right, from the receptor's perspective.

The two columns suggest that two participants form the evangelical transaction and stress what each participant does to enable Christ's redemptive work to take place. That is, the church is called (1) to proclaim and teach and dramatize (through the sacraments) the gospel, (2) to offer opportunities for contagious Christian fellowship, and (3) to serve people and the world while providing opportunities for seekers to join in service. This is what a contagious congregation has to offer. When it offers these resources in indigenous forms—using the language and adapting to the culture and needs of the target population, Christ can move clearly and powerfully through the outreach ministries of such a church.

The response of the receivers is crucial. They must at some stage commit their lives, hearts, and futures to following Jesus the Christ, their Lord. But one does not simply go out and "meet Jesus." He usually mediates his presence through the three resources. That is, he comes to us (and we meet him) through the Word, the believing fellowship, and the neighbor in need (Matt. 25:40).

Incidentally, an understanding of the four turnings by which people can appropriate the resources of the gospel will help explain most of those "problem people" in your congregation. Such people have taken one turn, but not the other three.[5]

This model of the four turnings helps us to see why part of our mission field is within the church or within the population of nominal (but undiscipled) Christians. Use the model in your church and public ministry, explain it to your people again and again—that they might really perceive the turnings their neighbors still need to take to become actual disciples.

I wish I could adequately dramatize what happens to people when they become involved with a contagious congregation's message, fellowship, and service and thereby become informed, supported, and serving Christian disciples. But perhaps one story will sufficiently dramatize the super reality of what I've been trying to lay out.

Several years ago I was leading a weekend evangelistic mission for a church community in a western Texas town. One night the soloist failed to show up, so the song leader unilaterally invited "testimonials" from the congregation. The first several testimonies were prototypes of the stereotype—rooted far in the past, obviously embroidered through many such retellings, and encrusted with the most banal of clichés.

Then a man stood up and rescued this sterile situation. He was an educator in the community, articulate and respected. He was also hunchbacked, and his face had been badly deformed since birth. I remember his words almost exactly (I have added his turnings parenthetically):

I'd like to take this opportunity to thank Christ and this Church for all that has happened in my life in the last ten years.

Let me explain what I mean.

It was ten years ago this month that a Sunday school class in this church took me in. I found a welcome, an affirmation, a support and strength from these Christians (koinonia) that I had found nowhere else in the community—including bars. Ours has always been a really studying Sunday school class—the Bible and contemporary Christian books. Soon I could put some of this stuff in my own words—though I'd not yet mustered the courage to do it for someone else's sake (kerygma). And we've always been a class with service projects—we campaigned for open housing, we provide partial support for several indigent families, every man is a "big brother" to some boy without a Dad living at home (diakonia). I got real involved in all of this.

After a bit more than a year of this I got up one morning and looked in the mirror. I discovered something within me that had never been there before and has never left me since. That morning I discovered within myself the power to love and accept myself—and ever since that morning I have been a free man. I thank Christ and all of you for that freedom.

That is just one example of what I mean when I say that evangelism is what Jesus Christ does through the Church's kerygma, koinonia, and diakonia to set people free.[6]

The contagious congregation's supreme and holy privilege is to offer countless people the call to discipleship and the means of a transformed identity and liberated life in Christ. So I invite you and your church to add extensively to the shelves of biographies of grace. I believe that every human being has the inalienable right to have the opportunity to follow Jesus Christ through a congregation and so discover Christian freedom. That is one reason why I am a Christian evangelist, and I devote this book to the real possibility that *your congregation* can become genuinely contagious.

CHAPTER II

A NEW MODEL FOR CHRISTIAN WITNESSING

If the evangelistic mission of lay Christians to undiscipled people is to be effective, the great possibility will be mediated as lay Christians befriend and serve others, and as they articulate the faith and hope that burn within them. This sharing, however, is checkmated by a widespread problem. Most of our lay people are inarticulate, even mute, when opportunities arise to verbally share the faith-possibilty with other people. They feel threatened. They fear they will freeze in the very act of attempting to witness to a friend or colleague. Devoted parishioners offer to do "anything but that!"

Some Christians feel very guilty about this weakness in their discipleship. They have heard pulpit anecdotes about non-Christians and Christians, the former assuming after years of contact with Christians that there must be nothing in it really—for if there were, and it was all that important, surely the Christians would have said something about it by now!

I do not begin this way to rebuke our lay people.

Christian lay people do maintain an effective Christian presence in their world. In many ways they are the salt of the earth, the light of the world, and the leaven which provides cohesion in the community. This Christian presence is important but not enough, because "Faith comes by hearing the Word of God." Faith is not an infectious disease. People without it do not "catch" it merely by being with someone who has it. To be sure, the Word is lent credibility through caring service and finds its contagion through fellowship, but the Word must be uttered and interpreted so that human beings have the live option of getting *their minds* around it and betting *their lives* upon it. Most of our people have a presence in the world, but they do not proclaim the gospel or persuade many people to become Christian disciples.

There is another problem in modern lay evangelism. Some lay Christians are *too* articulate. They jump in and sling texts before relating to persons and earning the perceived right to share. Their witness is perceived as a rehearsed totalitarian agenda which approaches all persons the same way, forcing everyone into the same cultural-religious mold. There is enough truth in this perception to hurt. Almost always, a degree of trusting friendship must be established before effective witness can take place (many zealots violate this principle.) And always, the form of our witness must be indigenous— fitting the other person's culture, language, needs, and response patterns.

All of this is written out of the recently growing realization that the USA and most of the rest of the western world is a mission field—in the traditional sense. As with all mission fields, the church's essential task is to fashion approaches that are indigenous and effective in this particular missionary setting among undiscipled

Americans. So, a new, conscious approach to interpersonal evangelism is a towering need today. Such an approach must have theological fidelity, and Christ-centeredness, and rootage in the New Testament. At the same time, it must be incarnational, elastic, and indigenous—relating to people where they are and as they are, rather than as we would like them to be. An incarnational approach that is radically open to human beings will enable them to hear the gospel as good news rather than strange propaganda—enabling response and new discipleship.

As you survey the literature of interpersonal evangelism, you will find that there is no tight consensus in the evangelical world on how to go about sharing the gospel interpersonally. But there is naive, near consensus in the widespread assumption that most (or all) people who become Christians do so as a result of a Christian stranger witnessing to them during a single visit, inviting them to accept Christ, and eliciting a saving decision—all in one transaction. This assumption is naive at two points. First, most people become Christians as a result of the cumulative effect of many evangelical transactions over a period of time. Second, while most persons who become Christians receive communication and invitation from a credible Christian, that Christian is much more often a relative or close friend than a stranger, the conversation is often spontaneous rather than preplanned—and very often the Christian suggests the gospel but does not fully articulate it, taking the new person to another Christian, class, worship service, or other meeting in which the great news is explained.

Nevertheless, much intentional witnessing must take place, and literature on evangelism offers many models and methods for consideration. Yet, underneath the variety, most of the literature teaches essentially two basic approaches that are analogous to the two ways of logical thinking—deduction: beginning general and moving particular, and induction: beginning particular and moving general.

THE DEDUCTIVE MODEL
OF CHRISTIAN WITNESSING

The deductive model is the more prevalent in the literature of evangelism. It takes many forms, generally emphasizing three stages. (1) The witnesser announces a general gospel to the person with whom he is sharing. (2) The witnesser appeals to this person for an umbrella commitment to the general gospel that has been shared. (3) It is presupposed that if the person accepts this general gospel, he or she will later work out the implications of this commitment throughout his or her life.

This is the way the process *used* to work. In the Second Great Awakening in America, during the early 1800s, the great evangelist Charles Grandison Finney preached a general version of the gospel to hosts of people who attended his tabernacle meetings. In thousands of cases, when they left these meetings they left not only committed Christians, but also committed abolitionists. That is, not only did they hear the general gospel, but they also saw its particular implications for the greatest social evil of their time.

But, it is precisely at this point that this deductive process breaks down in many lives today. Our churches are populated with people who have made an umbrella commitment to the Gospel, but have never worked out the specifics of that gospel in areas of life such as war, race relations, or economic practice. The deductive process is partly at fault. It is no longer indigenous to the mental processes of many American peoples and sub-cultures. An inductive approach would be more indigenous to more people.

BEGIN WITH HUMAN MOTIVES

Effective communication of the gospel begins with a demonstration of its relevance. England's Donald Lord Soper exclaims, "We must begin where people are, rather than where we would like them to be." By this he means that *the* point of contact between people and the gospel is people's needs, hopes, yearnings, fears, longings, and deepest motives. To be sure, human beings have many motives, but Christianity is armed with a multi-faceted gospel, and every basic human need or motive is matched by some distinguishable facet of the gospel—which is one reason why the gospel is good news.

Paul Tillich once said, "Almost every person you meet is fighting a great battle within." The evangelizer's job is to find the theater of that battle, to fashion a battle plan, and marshall the appropriate Christian resources for the engagement. In other words, "We must scratch where people itch," begin with their needs. This strategy, which rhetoricians call "the motivational appeal," was basic to Christianity's effectiveness from the the very beginning in the early church's excursions into the Roman Empire.[1] We must rediscover this strategy today.

A PHILOSOPHY FOR APPEALING TO MOTIVES

There are ethical *principles* for appealing to human motives. For one thing, a Christian who understands human nature knows that most people know what they want, but they may not know what they need. So, when the Christian hears people's wants and desires expressed, he must function as a diagnostician to determine the underlying motives for which the conscious wants are symptomatic.

Furthermore, the Christian is not ethically free to offer the gospel to fulfill just any need or desire that people might feel. There are many intrinsic needs and motives that human beings have simply because they are human—such as the desire for meaning, life beyond death, or to be loved and to love—and in relation to these needs the Christian may indeed offer the gospel as fulfillment, but there are some things that people want because they are sinners. These are not intrinsic human needs at all, but wants that originate in man's fallenness—wants such as a greed for money, or a passion for inordinate power over other people. In response to people's sinful wants, the Christian does not offer the gospel to fulfill those desires, but rather to eradicate them.

One's philosophy of motive appeals must also account for the varied response that different members of an audience will have when an appeal is made to a particular human motive or need. Keith Miller, in *The Becomers,* reports such an episode:

One time after I had spoken to an adult class which I had been teaching for some months, a man came up to me and said, "Good lesson! I think that was the first time I really heard the Gospel," and he actually seemed to mean what he said. But a few seconds later someone else in the same group commented (with at least equal sincerity) "Well, you've taught some good ones, but that one really missed. It just didn't sound like the Gospel! Besides, people aren't interested in the problems you talked about any more."[2]

MASLOW'S HIERARCHY OF HUMAN MOTIVES

I believe, as does Miller, that the Hierarchy of Human Motives as fashioned by Abraham Maslow provides great help for people who use motivational appeals in evangelism.[3] The hierarchy can be gridded as follows:

      7. Aesthetic needs
      6. Desire to know and understand
. . . .
      5. Need for self-actualization
      4. Esteem needs
         a. self-esteem
         b. esteem from others
      3. Love and belongingness needs
      2. Safety needs
      1. Physiological needs

Maslow's basic point in his theory and model is that *all* seven of these needs are intrinsic to human personality—but not all of them are center stage, in the forefront of consciousness, and *currently* motivating a person's life. The need that is in the forefront of consciousness and that is currently motivating the individual will be the lowest need that is basically unfulfilled.

For instance, the basic, rock bottom human needs are physiological—nutrition, elimination, sex, sleep. If these needs are not met, a person spends most of his time in an attempt to fulfill them; and until these physiological needs are met, he ignores his other needs that are present in the background of his personality. In wartime, when people are starving and homeless, they do not expend much energy asking philosophical questions or painting landscapes.

However, if a person's basic physiological needs are met, but his safety needs are not—they become the theater of his conscious and motivated life. People desire security, stability, freedom from fear, anxiety, and chaos. They prefer the familiar, they want predictability and order in their lives. They want to know that the rug is not going to be pulled out from under them. If they are insecure, they will work to achieve security.

But if they are secure, then their motivated activity shifts "upward" to satisfy their needs for love and belongingness. At this level, they desire love and affection in meaningful relationships, and they seek a reference or peer group with which to identify and in which they feel they belong.

When a person's needs for love and belongingness are essentially satisfied, then the need for esteem takes center stage. At this level, people seem to crave esteem from others. They desire reputation or prestige or status, or at the very least attention, recognition, or appreciation. At this level, people are also searching for self-esteem. They want to feel the kind of self-affirmation that only comes as a by-product of what they believe to be significant achievement, accomplishment, and competence.

When a person's need for esteem from himself and others is basically met, then his motivated behavior becomes "self-actualizing." At this "highest" level on the heirarchy, people work to realize their inner potential. They act to fulfill their destiny, to realize the purpose for their birth, and to express their individuality. Maslow's own words are instructive here: "A new discontent and restlessness will soon develop, unless the individual is doing what he, individually, is fitted for. . . . What a man can be he must be."[4]

Two other needs are intrinsic to human personality. (They are placed "above" the hierarchy, because the actual hierarchy stops with the need for self-actualization.) One is the need to know and understand—that thirst within for knowlege—to understand life and history, to have a satisfying world view. This need is not as neatly placed in the hierarchy as are the preceding ones, since it seems to pervade the two or three higher layers in the hierarchy. That is, once people's physiological and safety needs are met, they seem to jointly pursue the fulfillment of their need for a worldview and understanding as well as persuing fulfillment of affiliative, esteem, and self-actualization needs.

Maslow lists aesthetic needs as a basic area of human motivation, too. He was not certain that all people in fact have aesthetic needs, but he said, "I have at least convinced myself that in some individuals there is truly a basic aesthetic need, satisfied only by beauty."[5]

HOW TO USE
MASLOW'S HIERARCHY IN EVANGELISM

How can Maslow's hierarchy of human motivation be used by the practicing evangelizer? First, the would-be witnesser must immerse his mind in Maslow's scheme. It is a component of communication theory that does not help you if you learn it, it only helps you if you overlearn it. You must become so familiar with this hierarchy that you begin to think and function within the categories automatically, just as you now write a sentence without having to think consciously of nouns and verbs. Second, the witnesser's first task in evangelistic conversation is to determine where the other person is in his motivated life.

When the witnesser talks to a prospective Christian, he will discover that the needs and desires that the person expresses usually are only symptoms of the more basic, underlying needs that drive his life. He will also discover that expressed needs are almost always more specific than the general terms used in Maslow's scheme. For instance, a person will not be likely to say, "My self-esteem needs are deprived," but rather something like, "I never seem to accomplish what I set out to do." He will not say, "My need for esteem from others is unfulfilled," but rather, "The fellows at work never seem to notice me."

I have found that Maslow's model of human motivation can be especially useful in combination with the three basic resources in the gospel—message, fellowship, and service. Keith Miller's failure to rely on all three gospel resources may be the biggest problem with his use of Maslow's hierarchy. In *The Becomer's* Miller unduly stresses the Christian message to satisfy human beings at all seven levels of motivation, an exercise which proves to be very uneven in its effectiveness. Alone, the strength of the message is relatively impotent at two or three of the motivational levels. But when Christians approach others using all three resources, they have the power to engage any person redemptively at whatever level of motivation he is now struggling to satisfy.

THE INDUCTIVE MODEL OF
CHRISTIAN WITNESSING

Whereas the deductive process of evangelism begins with the general and moves to the particular, the inductive model begins with the particular and moves to the general. It has four basic stages: (1) The witnesser discovers, or the other person shares, some particular *need* for which the gospel is relevant. (2) The witnesser then shares a particular point or *facet* of the gospel that is relevant to the need. (3) The witnesser appeals to the person for a commitment—*response to the facet* that has been shared. (4) The witnesser knows that *God will be involved* in the process of evangelization. Knowing that everything does not depend on him—that God promises to do his part in evangelization—he has faith that after the prospect has had one or two particular experiences in Christian commitment, he will "taste" what Christianity has to offer human beings. As a result of the witness, the prospect now has a beachhead of experience from which he can decide whether to respond to a more general explanation of the gospel and to a more general appeal for commitment at some later point, say days or weeks later.

Recently I have refined this basic inductive approach into two operational models: an Inductive-Grace model and an Inductive-Mission model. The necessity for this conflation was caused by my struggles with the writings of Dietrich Bonhoeffer, especially his contentions about modern man having "come of age," in *Letters and Papers From Prison.*[6] One contention that has intrigued me for years is that we must learn to speak to human beings not so much in their weakness as in their strength.

As a doctrine of man, this suggestion does not survive

close examination. According to Maslow, there are very few people that are strong in the sense of being so complete and self-realized that they do not stand in any need of what we believe that the resources of the Christian faith have to offer. And yet, Bonhoeffer's point is valid. Some people are *relatively* weak, i.e., they have needs which are lower down on Maslow's hierarchy (these are the levels that traditional evangelism has usually engaged with some success—such as safety and love needs). Also, some people are relatively strong, i.e., if their lower needs in the hierarchy are presently fulfilled, and the motives that now dominate their lives—such as esteem and self-actualization needs—are higher up on Maslow's hierarchy. The problem is that these higher needs are not the conscious needs which evangelism, as usually done, can meet, because we are used to engaging people at their love needs and (especially) their safety needs. A renewed evangelism will engage the higher needs too.

Although Bonhoeffer's "strong man" theme is instructive, it is not intrinsically reliable, because the status of a "strong" person on Maslow's hierarchy is never totally secure. Find the strongest person in your community and celebrate his achievement, but also know that one day something may happen that will render him as weak (as low on the hierarchy) as any child, octogenarian, or invalid. *The great mandate for modern evangelism is to find people where they now are on the hierarchy of motives and to engage them at the appropriate level.* The strategy that I am leading to is this: When we find that people are relatively low on the hierarchy, we may engage them out of an Inductive-Grace model; when we find that they are relatively high on the hierarchy, an Inductive-Mission model.

THE INDUCTIVE-GRACE MODEL

The Inductive-Grace model is designed to approach human beings who are relatively weak, on the lower levels of Maslow's hierarchy. Perhaps some of their safety needs are not met or they still long for the assurance that they are loved or they want to be sources of love or they feel alienated and they desire to belong to some group or movement that will give them a sense of identity within a community.

When you find a person who represents a particular form of one of these needs, the grace model is operative. This model functions in four stages: (1) You establish a relationship of trust with the individual, and in the context of this established fellowship you discover or the person shares some need for which a facet of the gospel is relevant. (2) You then share and explain that facet of the gospel that is relevant to the need now driving this person. (3) You appeal to the person to open his being and to receive this particular resource of the gospel at this particular point in his life. (4) You trust that if the person does respond, God will honor the process and the person will indeed taste the grace of God. At another stage some days or weeks later, this person may well be open to a fuller explanation of the grace of God and might be very open to an appeal to live his whole life by the grace that he has begun to discover.

How would this model express itself in a concrete situation? Imagine a woman who lost her husband some four months ago. She confesses, "Sometimes I get so lonely I could climb these walls." First, tell her there is a God who loves her so intimately that the very hairs on her head are numbered. This God is personal, and she can pray to him. He is present and struggling with her,

A New Model   47

and desires a covenant-fellowship with her. The appeal: "Would you like to begin a devotional life? May I bring by a copy of *The Upper Room* for you to read regularly?"

Second, commend to her the gospel of koinonia; tell her about the koinonia group which meets every first and third Thursday night in a home just two blocks away. In this group people share with one another and really get to know one another intimately. They become, as Paul put it, "members one of another." They receive strength from one another and give strength to one another. "I know that they would welcome you as a member of their group. Would you like to go to their meeting next Thursday night? You need not give me an answer now. I'll call you in a few days."

THE INDUCTIVE-MISSION MODEL

The Inductive-Mission Model is offered as an effective approach to people who are relatively strong. Notice, again, even "strong" persons are not complete and totally fulfilled. They are still motivated and seeking human beings who happen to be higher on Maslow's hierarchy, a fact for which we give thanks. Their physical needs are basically met, they feel secure, they are not "stroke deprived," they have a sense of belonging and identity, perhaps they are highly regarded by others. But they are still motivated by the need for self-affirmation or for self-realization or to know and understand their lives.

The Inductive-Mission model differs from the Inductive-Grace model in one fundamental respect. Whereas the grace model directly engages some need or motive that now controls the life of a "weak" person, the mission model talks to a prospective Christian about a need that someone else has or a need in the community. The reason for this difference lies not only in the fact that other people's needs should be served and people who are "strong" are free to serve, but also because the higher motivational needs are not met by ministry from another, but rather as a *by-product* of a person's own Christian service. It is as you make your own life count that you are set free to esteem yourself, and it is in altruistic serving activities that we are set free to realize our potential to its height and to fulfill the reason for our birth.

The Inductive-Mission model proceeds in three sequential stages. (1) We share a certain Christian cause(s), with its christological intepretation, involving the need(s) of persons or the community. We might even present this person with a list and explanation of "the ten ministries that our church is engaged in for the sake of other people in the community." Notice that these causes must always be shared with an accompanying christological interpretation. That is, we share our conviction that Christ is working in our midst and in our community for these causes. He is seeking to redeem human beings and to bring health to them, and he is calling us to follow him in these enterprises.

(2) We appeal to the person, "Will you join Christ and us in one of these causes?" We can freely tell the person that he need not decide now. We will call again in several days to see if he has been able to arrive at a decision and to perhaps answer any questions that might have arisen in the meantime.

(3) At this final stage, we hedge our bets again—that God will not let us or the Word down, and that he will be involved in the message and the prospect's decision. So we believe that if our friend will respond to the challenge

and participate in Christ's mission, that he will thereby "taste of the Kingdom of God" and that experience will be self-authenticating. Then later on, perhaps days or weeks hence—but all of this must take place in measurable time—he will know whether the second, more general appeal to commit the rest of his life to Christ's kingdom is a decision he wants to make. It may take two or three experiences of being involved in Christian mission and subsequent reflection on those experiences to give a person the kind of background he needs for that serious overall commitment.

Extensive observations of persons becoming Christians reveal that most people who become Christians do so by an inductive process, so this new strategy is not novel or untested. We are reading what God would teach his outreaching church by observing how he is already working to create faith in persons. For instance, several years ago I met a woman who was a student at the Boston University School of Theology. She seemed very serious and devoted. She shared the story of how she came to be a Christian. Back in college she came to believe very much in the Civil Rights movement. She and a roommate decided to join Martin Luther King and his people in the now historic march from Selma to Montgomery. During the first day and a half of that march she felt something very strange and awesome and wonderful happening within her. It seemed as though she was in touch with Something that she had never been quite in touch with before. She mustered the courage to approach Dr. King and asked him what was happening to her. He replied, "I cannot be sure, but I believe that in these experiences Christ is making his approach to you." Some weeks later she did become a conscious Christian, and after graduating from college she went to seminary and today is a devoted minister of Christian education in a strong United Methodist church. Do you see what happened? Initially she became involved with a particular cause of Christ and his church. Fortunately, the experience was given a christological interpretation, and a seed was planted. The seed of new faith grew, and later—in measurable time—that particular beginning flowered into a splendid Christian.

HOW TO BEGIN WITH PEOPLE

A major hangup for many Christians focuses on the actual initiation of evangelistic conversations. They feel that if they could only get started and define the agenda without hopelessly bungling things or alienating the prospective Christian, then they could make it from there.

How you begin is probably not as crucial as anxious Christians seem to think, but it is a fairly important variable. There should be no stock or rehearsed or mechanical way of approaching human beings. We need to be elastic, willing to discover people where they are and as they are, and begin from there.

Some examples might help. Richard Armstrong, the author of *The Oak Lane Story,* was asked, "How did you teach people to begin evangelistic conversations?" He replied that he did not teach the witnessing laymen in his church any stock or stereotyped way to begin. He stresses the importance for the witnesser in those preconversation moments to trust in the Holy Spirit to give him the words to say, rather than trusting some verbal prescription. But, there was one opening question that most of his people used more often than any other: "How can we be of help to you?"

Armstrong suggests some advantages in this kind of opening. First, it is not an opening—such as "Are you saved?"—that people are used to and therefore innoculated against. Second, it is a question that does not easily permit a yes-or-no answer, but rather a considered response—and is therefore the kind of question that frequently leads to a very meaningful conversation.

One more point about how to begin in the Grace model will suffice. One year when I taught at the Perkins School of Theology, SMU, a colleague, Ronald Sleeth, brought several young women by and asked if they might visit my class. As I surveyed the dozen or so young men in the class, most of whom were bachelors, they quickly urged me to admit the visitors before they changed their minds! The women had recently moved to Dallas to begin an evangelistic community. After the class I asked a young woman from Great Britain the following question: "What is your methodology for approaching a secular non-Christian cold turkey?" She replied, "Huh?" I reminted my question: "Let's imagine that I'm sitting in a soda shop at the counter, and you walked in. You see me, and though you do not know me, you perceive that I am blue, that I am really depressed about something. How would you approach me?" She replied, "Why, I would walk up to you very gently and kindly, and I would say: 'Say, you look blue, like you're really depressed about something. Want to talk?' " The fellows exclaimed, "How about that! How very natural and obvious!" None of us will ever be able to forget that lesson—that the way you begin with people is in the most natural, warm, and humane way that you can think of in the concreteness of the moment.

An example of starting off with the Inductive-Mission model may be helpful. A pastor in Great Britain asked shopkeepers "What do you believe the church should be doing in this community to help people?" He received some plausible and even impressive suggestions from a large number of people. His quarterly church conference looked over the suggestions, discussed them, and finally settled on several as priorities for that community of faith. The pastor then went back to the people who had made these particular suggestions and asked them, "Will you join us in the expression of this ministry?" A fair number of them did respond, and several of them later joined the church on profession of faith.

BEGINNING AT THE MIDDLE

With many people though it is not necessary to begin from scratch. Sometimes it is possible for the lay evangelist to "begin at the middle." In the life history of most persons, God has not left himself without witness or withdrawn all possible initiatives toward a person until that wonderful day when you or I walk up that person's front steps to knock on the door! Indeed, it is very likely that you are not the first Christian that has ever shown an interest in this person. This means there may very well be some things in this person's history that you can bring to the forefront of his consciousness and build on it in the present. Dr. Samuel Southard stresses that we must not ignore the religious history of persons.[8] Use your conversation as an opportunity to bring positive experiences from a person's past back into consciousness again. Encourage them to tell you about their past.

For instance, "beginning at the middle" with the

Inductive-Grace model, you might ask a person such questions as, "How has God helped you in the past? What experiences have you had where you were helped to get through something and felt that Someone was guiding you? What experiences have you had where you made an improbable decision, but one that was nevertheless the right decision, and now as you look back you conclude that surely God's providential care was present for you?" Once a person has talked freely and at some length, including on an emotional level, and has affirmed again such experiences with a Christ-like God, you may then ask such questions as, "Has this God proven that he is worthy of your more complete trust? Do you desire to open your whole life to him?"

Employing the Mission model, and "beginning at the middle," you might ask a person, "What causes or services have you been involved in that you believe were very significant—causes that Christ would have been involved in if he had been here?" If you get a positive response you might ask, "Did you find this to be an intrinsically meaningful investment of a chunk of your life? Did you feel more fulfilled during this involvement than you have at most any other time in your life? Do you perhaps sense a Presence who is working in history and in human experiences to rescue and liberate people? Have you ever considered giving your whole life to the purposes of Christ for people?"

QUALIFYING THE INDUCTIVE MODEL

I have just presented a model. It is not a full-blown theory, but rather a simplistic explanation of the approximate way the process frequently works, a model that you can hold in mind as you reach out to people. I want to emphasize, however, that sophisticated use of any model involves an awareness of its limitations and exceptions.

For instance, this model neglects some of the factors involved in interpersonal witnessing. In an effort to stress and underscore some very important points, other principles that are not central to this model, but should help inform your use of it, are mentioned later in the book.

Again, interpersonal evangelism is never as easy as a quick rehearsal of this model might suggest. The fact that we function inductively rather than deductively does not remove the psychological "threat" in the gizzard of the witnesser, for the stakes are still high and much rides on these evangelical transactions.

Again, a transaction between a Christian and a not-yet Christian may not begin as quickly as this model seems to suggest. The model presupposes that friendship has been established prior to much gospel sharing. Unless we first relate to people, and they see that we are not religious cranks and that we are not on denominational Indian raids collecting spiritual scalps—they will be deaf to what we say.

Most important, the process of evangelizing works itself out within a person over a more extended period of time than a briefly stated model connotes. To use a metaphor, there must be a planting, and then a germination period, and then subterranean growth before visible flowering of new life. In other words, there will most likely be a period of searching, considering, struggling—a process that Christian witnessers nourish with *repeated* communications, visits, and social sup-port—until a person comes to terms with what he will do with Jesus who is called the Christ.

Communication theorists call this struggle the adoption process.[9] Theories about this process seek to answer the question, "What happens in a person's mind between the time when an idea or cause is initially introduced into his consciousness, and the time when he affirms that idea or cause and begins living his life in the light of it?" Communication theorists posit a five-stage process going on in a person's mind—a process which I have revamped slightly in accordance with my own understanding of evangelistic communication. The five stages are: awareness, relevance, interest, trial, and adoption.

The words almost suggest what happens at each stage. In the *awareness* stage the message, idea, or cause first enters a person's perceptual view in such a way that he is now aware of it. It is now part of the content of his consciousness and is therefore one of the things that he can think about and reflect upon. The second stage, *relevance,* refers to the stage in the life history of the idea when a person perceives the relevance of the message for some strong need or motive within his own life. As a result of this perception he takes a more active *interest* in the possibility of adoption, i.e., he asks questions about the message, checks some books out of the library, etc. In the *trial* stage, he begins turning the possibility around in his mind. He imagines what his life might be like if he adopted the idea. Perhaps as a devil's advocate he starts advocating the idea over a cup of coffee during a break at the office, but he is not yet committed to it. The final *adoption* stage comes when a person has sufficiently explored and experimented with his new perception. It seems self-authenticating. He now embraces it in such a way that appears irreversible. Even this model is simplistic, for we know that the adoption of an idea or

The Contagious Congregation

program is not necessarily irreversible. The adoption can atrophy over time, which is one reason why a new convert must also be given continual nurture and social support if his adoption of the Christian possibility is to remain the central factor in his life for the rest of his life. In any case, the process from initial awareness to initial adoption *always* takes a while—certainly longer than one conversation, usually weeks, and sometimes months, occasionally years.

THE INDUCTIVE MODEL COMMENDED

I commend greater use of the inductive approach in interpersonal evangelism for this generation. I very much believe that this approach will be more effective in reaching millions of non-Christians in this generation. The inductive model is more indigenous to the ways secular people think, live, and reach important conclusions and decisions in their lives. We are a pragmatic and technological culture, and people reared in this culture tend to think pragmatically and specifically rather than in philosophical generalities. Besides, many people with whom we will speak have already been exposed to various versions of deductive evangelism. Many people have been innoculated by prior experiences and are now immunized against other deductive approaches.

I also believe that an inductive model for Christian witnessing is more natural to lay evangelizers because it is similar in structure to other familiar communication patterns from honest sales, to problem solving, to consulting and counseling. It is situational, elastic, adaptive, concrete. It enables us to indigenize our approach for the receiver. It enables us to be more radically open to the leading of the Third Person. We can train people in the inductive approach and reasonably challenge them to implement it.

Of course, the Inductive-Grace model and the Inductive-Mission model place a realistic burden upon Christians—we must still take the initiative. We do not have the luxury in a secular era to wait until people come to us, because millions of them never will. In our generation, as in the first one, the sower must "go forth" to sow the seed of God's Word.

Use of inductive processes also place realistic burdens on the local church. In light of the Grace model, we must be sure that the particular ministries and resources of the gospel that we offer to people really are the ministries and resources which can engage and meet basic human needs. In light of the Mission model, the local church must make sure that the causes which it offers people the opportunity to join really are Christian causes that Jesus would be doing, that really count, that would make a significant difference in people's lives or in the community's life if they were to prevail; causes that would fulfill human beings (giving them self-esteem and self-realization) if they were to become committed to them and involved with them.

We will not attract and fulfill people if all we offer them are the usual ecclesiastical chores and church activities—ushering, taking up the collection, serving on committees, going to meetings. Nor can we fool them by sticking avant-garde labels on the same old churchy bottles. I conclude with a negative example. I saw a congregation's Sunday bulletin. Half of the back was devoted to "Our Church In Mission." I was intrigued to find out what this church was doing "In Mission" for an entire week:

Today	2:00 P.M.	6th grade Sunday school class picnic at Snyder Park—meet at the church, bring money for activities at the park, swim wear and own hot dogs, hamburgers and buns. Each one may invite a friend.
	6:30 P.M.	Senior Hi UMYF swimming party at the home of Jim Fritz. Meet at the church at 6:30.
Tues.	8:00 P.M.	The Career Women's group will meet in the church parlor. A demonstration on tulle painting will be given by Mrs. Carrie Ford.

There is nothing wrong with these church activities. But there is not enough right with them! If these are the most meaningful involvements that we have to offer people, many of our present members will continue looking at the back door and most outsiders will continue ignoring our front door. But if we are willing to revamp our agenda, and make sure that most of the things we do are really engaging human needs and are really Christian causes, then we will capture the allegiance of great numbers of people who will want to follow Jesus Christ in the company of his disciples, because this is the most worthwhile and fulfilling enterprise among all of the options for service and self-giving that are presented to people in our culture.

A New Model   **59**

POSTSCRIPT
WHAT ABOUT COUNSELING SEEKERS INTO FAITH?

Several persons have pointed out that the Inductive model, as described above, gives more clarity to the task of helping people toward faith than *into* faith. How can we be counselors or "midwives" for seekers who are on the threshold of faith's experience and new life?

Here, I strongly commend the evangelistic counseling model of Canon Bryan Green in *The Practice of Evangelism.*[10] The following is a summary of his approach. The reader should by all means read Green himself on this crucial topic.

Canon Green's counseling method is for people "who have pursued the pathway towards Christ a certain distance" and are now subjectively ready for a decisive experience of Christian faith. Three guiding axioms are referred to the counselor before Green explains his method. (1) The counselor needs a "spiritual sensitiveness which enables him to see how God is leading a soul to himself." (2) "Once you have sat down for the talk, come to the point quickly" and "try and get the person to whom we are talking to interpret himself to himself and to see the way in which God is trying to lead him into conversation." (3) Personal honesty is important. If the counselor senses that "neither of us knows what to do next," he should articulate this so that moments of silence or mutual groping will not be embarrassing but useful.

The first of Green's four major principles for securing commitment from the advanced seeker is the establishment of a real sense of need. Green believes that when many people seek to become Christians they come out of a particular need such as fear of death, loneliness,

The Contagious Congregation

weakness of will, moral failure, specific sins, a lack of aim and purpose, or frustration in the face of evil in the world. Note: The evangelist must be able to convince the inquirer that his felt need is symptomatic of his basic need for a restored relationship with God and that only as this basic need is met will the felt symptomatic need be fulfilled.

The second of Green's principles of evangelistic counseling is *"the offer of Christ."* The offer should be extended in such a way that *acceptance* will meet both the *basic need for God* and the *symptomatic need* that motivated the original religious quest. Green recommends that the offer be explained with the help of the New Testament gospels—i.e., using some relevant passage or a story of how Christ met a need that either parallels or is analogous to the symptomatic need of the inquirer.

The third principle is the leading of the inquirer into *"the act of faith."* This is a two-sided act of the will which involves *"repentance"*—the seeker's willingness to drop all that blocks him from God and his best self—and *"faith"*—the opening of the self to God in an obedient trust. Canon Green believes that the best way to lead most persons into this act is to provide "a focus for their faith"—which is generally a passage of scripture. He often uses an invitational text such as Revelation 3:20—"Behold, I stand at the door and knock; if any man hear my voice and open the door I will come in." Green reads the text, very briefly explains its meaning, and emphasizes that the great issue is whether the seeker will open the door and let Christ into his life.

What happens next is crucial in the seeker's pilgrimage. Some persons should now be granted the opportunity to be quiet and alone, but usually it is "wiser to suggest that the seeker should make his response of faith to Christ immediately and in another's presence." The sequence of events that follows involves a style of counseling which is best dramatized in Green's own words:

I say, "Let's kneel down together that you may put your trust in Christ." It is very rarely that I ask the seeker to pray out loud. I want him to forget me at this sacred moment and to talk to God alone. Rather I do tell him that I want him to be alone with God and to open his life to Christ. I simply say, "Just tell me when you have finished praying." Then we are silent. I pray while he is praying. After a while he indicates that he has finished praying. Immediately I ask, "Has Christ really come to you?" or "Has God made Himself real to you?" or "Has He met your need?" If it is the work of the Holy Spirit and a real act of faith has been made, the answer is almost invariably something like, "Yes, I think so." My next question is equally important: "How do you know?" As I have tried to explain so carefully a few moments before that we must trust the promise of Christ and that it is not any feelings but what Christ says that matters, one would expect the answer to be something like, "Because Christ promised to come." Invariably the answer is quite different, on these lines, "Because I feel it," or "I know it." In other words, it is an experience that has come, an inward realization of Christ's presence that has been given. I always answer, "I am glad to hear it. Thank Him out loud." The instant response is a simple act of witness in a few words of thanksgiving. The simple words are very often only, "Thank you, Lord Jesus, for coming to me." At this point I pray. . . . "Lord, I thank You that You have come into his life and become his Savior and Friend. Help him to keep his eyes open to see what You tell him to do next, that he may know that You are leading him and may learn to trust You better. Amen."

The fourth principle is the *communication of* a sense of *"assurance* that God in Christ has taken hold of him, and that he has been reconciled to God." This communication comes in two stages. First, the evangelist carefully explains that the convert's assurance that God has accepted him and entered him does not rest upon his own emotions or subjective feelings, but "on the promise and character of God"; the cross of Christ is the sign of that promise and character. The second stage of this communication of assurance is continual—the Holy Communion. In this sacrament the believer remembers the fact of his own emptiness, and experiences Christ's act for, toward, and in him again and again and again.

CHAPTER III

A PROVEN MODEL
FOR COMMUNICATING
THE GOSPEL

In their outreach, Christians are called to communicate to people a very ancient treasure—the gospel of the apostolic church. They communicate the message of this treasure with the hope that people will be persuaded to accept that great news and become lifetime followers of Jesus through his church. This mission will become more effective when evangelizing Christians rediscover an ancient and proven model for communicating and persuading.

The Christian witnesser, of course, is in part a communicator. Communication does not exhaust evangelism, because evangelization takes place through koinonia and diakonia as well as kerygma. So the evangelist is a communicator, and a relator, and a servant/reformer. But, there is no effective evangelizing without effective and persuasive communication—for at least two reasons: (1) While the truth has its own intrinsic power, it needs the help of an effective human communicator to penetrate and convince the conscious-ness of a receptor.[1] (2) While it is the Holy Spirit who convinces people that "Jesus is Lord," He works through the human principles of persuasion.[2]

So, increasing numbers of Christians who want to reach out are asking, *"How* can we come to grips with the task of evangelistic communication? *How* can we become effective enablers of the Great Possibility for other people? Many resources in communication studies can help, but none more substantially than the most influential single model of speech persuasion in his-tory—Aristotle's model, found in his classic text, *The Rhetoric of Aristotle."* [3]

According to Aristotle's model, people are persuaded from resources in the speaker, the message, and the auditor—or, more specifically, the *ethos* of the speaker, the *logos* of the message, and the *pathos* of the auditor. The *ethos* of the speaker persuades when people, from what they perceive of the speaker's being and personali-ty, sense that they can trust him. The *logos* of the message persuades when people find the content of the message and its supportive reasons and examples to be convincing. And the auditors are persuaded from their own *pathos* when the speaker, through his message and personality, engages people at the points of their deepest *motives* and/or when he engages or arouses in them *emotions* that are conducive to the acceptance of his message.

I believe that it is possible to use Aristotle's model and categories for planning more effective evangelical communication—allowing for supplementary insights from other rhetorical schools, modern studies of persuasion, homiletics, and evangelism.

THE MESSAGE

First, people are persuaded by the logos of the message. The Christian evangelist is entrusted with a message "once delivered to the saints." Getting that message and its claims upon people across is basic in Christian evangelism. Unfortunately, some evangelists skip this task and appeal for a response from people on the basis of what they already believe. They invite people to become Christians without *first* proclaiming and interpreting the gospel. This is at best a naive and counterproductive exercise, because what people believe is often mere civil religion or folk wisdom dressed in Christian clothing. At worst, an appeal of response without proclamation and interpretation is a form of ecclesiastical totalitarianism that exploits people's emotions and engineers a contract without their adequate awareness of what they are getting into and why. So true evangelism involves faithful *message* sharing. And to be faithful and effective, the message should be (1) relevant, (2) clear, and (3) biblical.

For the message to be perceivably relevant, Christian witnessing to non-Christians must begin with a demonstration that the Christian message really has something to do with the deepest needs and motives of human beings. Unfortunately, the proverbial "man in the street" is convinced that Christianity is merely an otherworldly soul-saving enterprise whose preoccupations in this world are limited to ecclesiastical affairs, doctrinal squabbles, elitist liturgies, potluck suppers, and rummage sales. He believes that Christianity is OK for the little old ladies of both sexes who like churchy things, but that

Christianity is irrelevant to life and to the real issues and struggles that preoccupy and haunt human beings—like insecurity, alienation, and failure, the breakdown of intimacy, and his not-OK feelings and lack of fulfillment. The Christianity he perceives has nothing to do with his dignity, oppressive environment or war or injustice or crime. He sees politicians using religion for their partisan ends, rather than religion influencing the political and economic affairs and institutions upon which the people depend. He does not see the Christian faith making any difference in "real" life.

Great Britain's Donald Lord Soper—the most experienced Christian advocate in our lifetime to secular unchurched people—contends that "we must begin where people are, rather than where we would like them to be." He commends a strategy that begins with people, their issues, their social problems, and their crises. By such an initiative we win a hearing, and we show that Christianity is intrinsically involved with the deepest human concerns as well as obviously religious concerns. If Christianity is a redemptive approach to life as a whole, we must demonstrate this. Following this initial demonstration of relevance, Soper then offers a *theological* analysis of the condition or problem he is engaging and proclaims and interprets Christianity and its mission as the redemptive approach that people can discover.[4]

Second, the witnesser's message must be clear. Now, everyone knows that, or thinks he does. Yet, many Christians who would be the first to acknowledge this principle are the most obscure in their own communication. Christians who mean to be clear can become more clear when they arrive at an adequate understanding of the nature of rhetorical clarity.

Two key elements are involved in producing clarity;

one is *language*. The language we use must be immediately clear to the target audience. Every word must be intelligible, in the context in which it is spoken. Unfortunately, pastors and lay people who are interested in evangelism seem to be almost universally afflicted with an oral disease which causes them to speak either pious platitudes or technical theological jargon, both of which strike most people with the clarity of a first-time exposure to Swahili. After all, not many outsiders have any clear or accurate reference for most of the stockwords within the Christian tradition: sin, justification, saved, blood, Kingdom of God, sanctification, etc. As Lawrence Lacour says, "We must remint our language or we will shortchange our hearers."

The other key principle to clear communication teaches that the content of what we say should be restricted to or focused on what persons can in fact undertand and assimilate in one oral transaction. Our frequent mistake in evangelism is to try to say too much in one sermon or conversation which results in "information overload." That is, we sock 'em with more propositions, ideas, or verses than they can get their minds around or assimilate and digest at one time. True, we have what Harold DeWolf calls a "multi-faceted gospel." But people have a "limited intake capacity." This frustration is only overcome when we purpose in any one visit or sermon to say only one or two things, to say them very well, and with adequate explanation and application. What we say should be determined at least in part by which facet of the gospel is most relevant to this person or group at that moment. One precaution: Do not share that one facet as if it were the whole gospel.

Third, the message must be biblical. We are the people of a Book, and the church is called into existence by the

Christ-event that Scripture bears witness to and interprets. As we study that Book, sometimes its events step off the pages and visit and reshape *our* history. In evangelism we purpose that the Christ-happening shall happen again in the beings of people who hear us. Outsiders know that whatever the Christian message is, it should be based on Christian scripture. So we must discover our message *there,* and not in our imaginations, nor our sub-cultures, nor even in the doctrines that we may have accepted as biblical from exposure to extrabiblical sources like theologians, pamphlets, etc.

We must receive our message from the Bible itself, and people must perceive that we get our message there. People are not acutely interested in our private opinions. Nor are they salivating to hear what modern theologians say. If they are interested in anything at all from the Christian storehouse, they are interested in what our Bible has to say and especially what Jesus himself taught. Indeed, some rank secular people may not be open to anything the Old Testament has to say, nor to John or Paul, because they associate all of this with a dogmatic tradition that they reject. But most secular people are still interested in what Jesus proclaimed and taught.

Now, stressing that we derive our message from the Bible, does not mean that we are obligated to use "Bible language." Quite the contrary, the biblical message is best understood in the common language of the people which *The Good News Bible* effectively models for us. But using the Bible does not mean that we stitch together selected texts in order to make the Bible say what we would like it to say. Our job is to discover and transmit what the Bible really does say, especially as it speaks to target auditor(s). This means that we must be engaged in our own beings in a continual dialogue with, and immersion in, that Book. Supremely, we are interpreters of Scripture to people, translating the facets of truth from that book and communicating them with relevance and clarity to people's lives.

THE AUDIENCE

Evangelistic messages are intended to engage *persons* where they are to elicit appropriate response. The strategy of adapting to one's audience does not mean that we compromise our message or fudge on it. It means that we begin where we discover people to be, that we adapt to the realities of the hearer's culture, moods, feelings, emotions.

Unfortunately, the subject of "emotional appeals" frequently reveals that many Christians, and especially pastors, have deep-rooted hangups. They cringe at the thought of arousing deep feelings within people. As one fairly eminent preacher once said to me, "I would not stoop so low!" But maybe we are called to reach so high.

This anti-emotional attitude originated in a now outdated school of psychology called faculty psychology. This school is several centuries old—quite pre-scientific—and has now been rejected by almost every thinking member of the human race except ordained ministers. Faculty psychology presupposed that the human cranium contains five separate compartments —each of which houses one of five faculties: intellect, emotion, will, memory, imagination. Speakers assumed that they could by design engage one compartment of a person's mind and not another. Later, clergymen came to feel that it is "good" to speak to people's intellect, but base to speak to people's emotions.

Well, modern psychology has eclipsed this primitive and mechanistic understanding of the human mind. And social psychologists in this generation have sabotaged it. True, you can helpfully describe human mental activity in terms of such basic tendencies as: thinking, feeling, willing, remembering, and imagining, but it is at present impossible to locate these faculties as compartments in the human brain. It is also impossible to pretend a neat and separate division between them. Indeed, one's beliefs and feeling are interrelated; when you change one, to some degree you change the other. If you want to change people's feelings, some persuasion theorists contend that you must change the beliefs that in part inform those feelings; and conversely, if you want to change people's beliefs, then change the feelings which are energizing their beliefs.

Rhetoricians have known for a long time that if you want to change beliefs, elicit response, and change attitudes and behavior, you had better arouse or induce appropriate feelings. According to George Campbell, who wrote *A Philosophy of Rhetoric* in 1776: "To say that it is possible to persuade without speaking to the passions is but at best a kind of specious nonsense."[5]

There is one qualifier: an appeal to the emotions should be at the service of the message. That is, to merely fish for an emotional response without helping people to understand the message is religious fascism. As Campbell wrote: "Passion is the mover to action; reason is the guide."[6] Reason informs and guides people's decisions and actions, but feeling energizes those beliefs and triggers and ignites a response.

Appropriate emotional arousal *enables* response.

There will be no religious response without it. Whatever decisions ordinary people reach, they decide more from feeling than from careful consideration of facts and logical procedure. Any teenage boy wishing to borrow his dad's car knows the strategic importance of the auditor's favorable feeling state—that is why he poses the request *after* supper. The good advocate who wants his cause to have a chance will engage or arouse in his audience a feeling state that is favorable, rather than hostile, to his cause. I once heard Martin Luther King say: "When I preach the Gospel I have two objectives. First, I want people to *understand* the message. Second, I want people to *feel* the message in their very bones." He contended that only when people both understand and feel the truth are you likely to get the response you desire. There is no persuasion without appropriate emotional arousal, but your appeal to people's emotions must be at the service of the message and not instead of it.

Well, how do we arouse appropriate feelings that are conducive to message acceptance? Three strategies are basic.

First, engage the hearer's conscious life motives. Wayne Minnick, in *The Art of Persuasion,* contends that emotions are related to motives, i.e., to what we desire, what we hope for, what we want.[7] People especially respond with feeling when they see that their motives are likely to be *frustrated* or *gratified.*

For example. A young woman wants a baby very much; she and her husband have been trying to start a family for several years. She visits her gynecologist; he examines her and states a scientific conclusion: "Martha, not only can you start a family, but you have conceived within the past five or six weeks." She leaps up, embraces him, plants a kiss on her doctor's cheek and rushes to telephone her husband. All the physician did in this case was to communicate a factual message that engaged a deep motive within her, and, in this case, promised gratification. As you speak to the deepest needs and wants of persons they will respond with appropriate emotion. So Cicero advised: "Orators must have a scent for an audience; for what people are feeling, thinking, waiting for, wishing."[8]

A second strategy for engaging or arousing the emotions that facilitates message acceptance is to personalize the message. We must help people see that the Christian gospel is not a routine proclamation to the universe in general as if we were speaking to a blur of human faces. Rather, they must see that the message of a seeking, gracious God is "for you." As Kierkegaard said, the gospel is like "a love letter from God with your personal address on it." William Warren Sweet wrote in his *Revivalism in America* that "To personalize religion is to emotionalize it."[9] Now, this strategem is no demigogical ploy. It is intrinsically rooted in the gospel of a God who knows us and loves us so intimately that the very hairs on our heads are numbered and who calls to us by name: "Adam, Adam, where are you?" Jesus also taught this through the parables of the lost sheep, the lost coin, and the two lost sons in Luke 15. We must recover this strategy of personalizing the message. When the auditor really senses that the eternal message is "For Me!" he is sufficiently emotionally involved to respond.

One of the frustrations of modern Christian communication is that many people have heard the personal message of a seeking God so often that it strikes them with the non-force of last month's news. Even the parables of Jesus in Luke 15 are received as old hat. Our challenge is to find fresh ways of interpreting this gospel, so as to enable people to hear it as though for the first time.

For example, Bishop Roy Nichols shares a modern parable about a young woman who went to see a psychiatrist. The doctor had established that she was a wife and mother of three children, and almost at random he asked, "Which of your three children do you love the most?" She answered instantly, "I love all three of my children the same." He paused. The answer was almost too quick, too glib. He decided to probe a bit. "Come, now, you love all three of your children the same?" "Yes, that's right," she said, "I love all of them the same." He said, "Come off it now! It is psychologically impossible for anyone to regard any three human beings exactly the same. If you're not willing to level with me, we'll have to terminate this session." With this the young woman broke down, cried a bit, and said, "All right, I do not love all three of my children the same. When one of my three children is sick, I love that child more. When one of my three children is confused, I love that child more. When one of my children is in pain, or lost, I love that child more. And when one of my children is bad—I don't mean naughty, I mean really bad—I love that child more. "But," she added, "except for those exceptions I do love all three of my children about the same."

Through this modern parable, Nichols is trying to say that the Christian faith represents a God who knows and loves you just as he knows and loves all other human beings on this planet—but with this addition: when you are sick or hurting or lost or confused or in pain or depraved—he loves you even more. So, we personalize the message that "God loves each one of us as if there were only one of us to love" (St. Augustine). If you employ this strategy, you will sometimes engage and arouse feelings in people that are appropriate to the message and which enable message acceptance.

The third major strategy is the revelation of your own feelings. Revelation is mediated through human personality, and is in small part the self-revelation of the witnesser. The witnesser is not mechanically reporting something that once happened for all people (but neither is he engaged in autobiograhical indulgence). He is reporting and interpreting something that he is personally involved with and that is changing his own life. He deeply wants people to hear the good news, and he is earnestly praying that people will embrace the possibility that the message carries to them, although he would never coerce them. So, when it is appropriate and when people would perceive it is genuine, the witnessing Christian may reveal his own feelings. Then sometimes, by the process called empathy, the prospective Christian will participate with him in the emotion. To this basic principle I hasten to add two qualifiers.

First, revealing your own feelings, especially in preaching or in speaking, is more appropriate near the end rather than at the beginning. If done at the beginning, it is more likely to be counterproductive—with the auditor regarding the speaker as losing control of himself. Second, you will more likely induce appropriate feelings within people when you only partly reveal your feeling state. That is, when people perceive that you are feeling something deeply and that you feel it even more deeply than you are allowing yourself to exhibit—*that* is when people make the empathetic leap and begin to identify with your feelings and with the power of your message.

THE COMMUNICATOR

The third major source of persuasion is the communicator's ethos. The bearer of the Word plays a significant role, especially in how he is perceived by the auditor. There is a folk maxim which exclaims: "What you are speaks so loudly I cannot hear what you say." That is close to Aristotle's principle. Aristotle would remint it to say "What you seem to me to be speaks so loudly that it influences my response to what you say." The crucial variable is not what the speaker actually is, but how he is perceived by the hearer. The hearer's perception of the communicator influences his reception of the message. There seems to be a mechanism operative in the auditor's mind. Perhaps subconsciously, the auditor is asking certain questions about the advocate, and the answers that surface will partly determine his response to the message. What are those questions? What is it that auditors want to know?

Some venture that auditors want assurance of a communicator's sincerity. On a certain level this is incontestable. The factor of sincerity is especially noticeable in its absence, whether in persons or populations. Fred Allen used to say that "you could take all of the sincerity in Hollywood and stuff it in a gnat's navel and leave enough room for two caraway seeds and an agent's heart!" Sincerity is a factor. But the substance of the speaker's ethos is more substantial and subterranean than merely his sincerity. Aristotle isolated three factors and called them: intelligence, character, and good will. He contended that those are *the* three factors—and it follows that if the hearers perceive the speaker as knowing what he is talking about, as being a good person, and as being well disposed toward them, then the speaker will consequently have the confidence of his hearers.[10]

Ethos theory needs some revision to inform Christian evangelism. One major factor in the ethos of the evangelizer is his perceived *expertise* (similar to Aristotle's intelligence criterion). Does the advocate know what he is talking about? Is he in a position to know? Has he done his homework? Does he speak with reasonable authority? Like many principles, this is sometimes best illustrated by a negative example. Notice a certain late night radio "evangelist," whom gullible people swallow unthinkingly, but whom most thinking people regard as a joke. When pronouncing on national and world affairs he claims to possess the answers, but he speaks in circles and never gets around to articulating those answers. Thinking people who look for expertise in advocates dismiss him as an ecclesiastical Barnum. Expertise is a key factor, and most auditors automatically try to determine whether the speaker possesses it.

The second major factor is identification. Some communication theorists contend that identification is the key to persuasion and that there is no persuasion without it.[11] In evangelistic communication, affirmative answers to three questions establish a feeling of identification in the auditor's mind: (a) "Is he one *of* us?" That is, is he "our kind of folk"? or is he "different" or "strange"? (b) "Is he one *with* us?" Does he share our hopes, our feelings, and our yearnings? (c) "Is he *for* us?" Or is he speaking for himself? Does he stand to get something out of this—is he trying to add numbers to the church roll? In short, is the witnesser speaking selfishly or out of altruism?

The third major factor in the witnesser's ethos is *credibility*. It is delineated by Helmut Thielicke in *The*

Trouble With The Church.[12] It has arisen with, and perhaps because of, commercial advertising. We see an athlete on a TV commercial attributing a revolution in his social life to the strategic application of a certain underarm deodorant, and we ask, "Does he really use Brand X, and has it made all that much difference in his social life, or is he just a paid propagandist for the Menren Company?" Likewise, we have witnessed the growing importance of credibility in politics, especially regarding election campaigners.

The contemporary search for credibility has been transferred to Christian preachers and to other Christians who attempt to represent the Christian message to people. People wonder, "Does this Christian really live in the house that he speaks from? Has he something ultimately significant? Or is he just a propagandist for the organized church?" Thielicke believes that the crucial issue is "the credibility of the witnesser."

This is corroborated by Dean Kelly who wrote *Why Conservative Churches are Growing.*[13] Kelly offers two reasons why certain chuches are growing in our time. First, conservative churches are growing because they presume to interpret "the meaning of life in ultimate terms." Second, those churches grow which make demands upon people, when their advocates seem to be making great sacrifices for the cause that they advocate. Kelly infers that most people are not sophisticated philosophers possessing the epistemological tools to evaluate the competing truth claims of Baptists, Moonies, Marxists, and many more. So, how do people determine, from a smorgasbord of religious truth claims, what to believe and what not to believe? They observe the various advocates, and they are more inclined to believe those advocates who are giving the most and sacrificing the most for the cause that they commend to others.

Decades ago, Ralph Waldo Emerson expressed the significance of credibility in these memorable words:

The reason why anyone refuses his assent to your opinion or his aid to your benevolent design, is in you. He refuses to accept you as a bringer of truth, because, though you think you have it, he feels that you have it not; you have not given him the authentic sign.[14]

CHAPTER IV

COMMUNICATING THE GOSPEL TO RESISTANT SECULAR PEOPLE

The communicating congregation inevitably discovers "resistant people"—folks who, at least for now, are not open to a life-change, do not "have the ears" to really hear the gospel—the kind of people William Booth characterized as "gospel proof."

One will not find much help in the evangelism literature of the Anglo-American tradition for either understanding or coping with resistant people. Our usual practice among them betrays our lack of an informed basis for reaching out to resistant secular people.

For instance, some evangelicals simply write them off, with rationalizations about their "hard hearts." Others resort to repetitive proclamation—without adaptation or explanation. Others withdraw from resistant people, vowing to return to them as soon as the denominational agency sends the packaged "perfect method" for making instant Christians out of seemingly resistant people.[1]

Some much-needed illumination on this problem comes from the Third World church growth research of Donald McGavran and his colleagues—who, on the basis of extensive data and many case studies, counsel *against* writing resistant people off, badgering them, or abandoning them. The authors bring an element of realism and a badly needed approach to strategy for Western churches.[2] Basically, McGavran teaches that receptivity and resistance ebb and flow in persons and peoples. People who are receptive now may be resistant later, and vice versa. The grand strategy (see next chapter) is to reach out to receptive people while they are receptive—that is the supreme way forward in church growth. But for resistant people, the policy is to hang in there with them in a mission of "presence," serving them as they will let us, saying what we can, with the long-haul policy of building bridges, plowing and planting for a later harvest, and making sure we are present for them and credible to them when they do turn more receptive. McGavran counsels that

abandonment is not called for. . . . No one should conclude that if receptivity is low, the church should withdraw mission.

Correct policy is to occupy fields of low receptivity lightly. They will turn receptive some day. . . . While they continue in their rebellious and resistant state, they should be given the opportunity to hear the Gospel in as courteous a way as possible. But they should not be swamped by Christians, lest they become even more resistant.

They should not be bothered and badgered. . . . Resistant lands should be held lightly.[3]

Note that the principle of indigenous outreach is always basic, whether among resistant or receptive peoples. The approach and method must "fit" people culturally—speaking their language and engaging their felt needs. So,

no single method will fit all populations. A primitive tribe needs one method, urban masses of Brazil another, and rural Filipinos in the barrios of Mindanao a third. Africans welcome one kind of congregation, Latin Americans a second, and men out of the tightly closed caste system of India still another.

Church growth in receptive populations is marked by particularity. Much confusion and loss are caused by forgetting this. Each population is a separate case, more different from other populations than one person is from another. Its nature conditions church growth. . . .

Each population, therefore, must have its own formula. Whole milk, so to speak, must be modified by the addition of different ingredients in different proportions. The essentials of the Gospel, the authoritative Bible, and the unchanging Christ remain the same for all populations. But the accompaniments can and must be changed freely to suit each particular case.[4]

All of the above generalities also apply to the pre-evangelizing of resistant people in western countries, like the U.S.A. But beyond these generalities, we do not know as much about resistant westerners as we now do about many resistant Third-World peoples, nor about how to pre-evangelize them. This chapter is devoted to filling part of the gap, based on actual case studies of effective evangelization among resistant people in Great Britain, and is offered with a special focus on a chief cause of resistance among western peoples—the phenomenon of *secularization* and its effect on western cultures—*secularity.*

Everyone knows we live in a secular age and communicate with secular people. Yet most people are fuzzy in their use of these terms. One person means one thing, another person means another. This ambiguity is unfortunate because these terms, rightly understood and taken seriously, provide a significant key to understanding and unlocking much of the mystery of the present age regarding the communication of the gospel in western countries.

Most serious Christians are aware that it is difficult to attract some people to the Christian faith. They have experienced this in trying to share the faith-possibility, but have not conceptualized the causes of the difficulty. Let us look at our western secular mission field in three parts: (1) the *basic* fact of our secular age, (2) generalizations about *secular* people that are the products of secularization, and (3) some major principles and strategies of communicating the gospel to secular resistant people.

THE BASIC FACT OF OUR SECULAR AGE

The widespread fact of secularity has resulted from a process called secularization. The secularization process is defined by sociologists and historians as follows: "the withdrawal of whole areas of life and thought from the control or the heavy influence of the church."[5] What this process means is best seen with historical perspective.

Throughout the Middle Ages, the church exercised control or heavy influence over all of Western culture, including every sector of life—personal and communal. A society was built on this arrangement of the church informing, influencing, and sometimes controlling every area of man's life and thought. This arrangement was called Christendom. Christendom lasted in some form for ten centuries, beginning after the conversion of

Constantine in the fourth century and lasting until the Renaissance and Reformation periods of the fourteenth and fifteenth centuries.

Now, the fact of the withdrawal of areas of life and thought from the control or heavy influence of the Church (secularization) is best seen through examples. Expressed abstractly, secularization is an elusive concept; but explained concretely, it becomes a self-evident and self-justifying emphasis for modern evangelism. During the Middle Ages the church had heavy influence in most areas of man's life, but as various areas of life and thought were withdrawn from the control or influence of the church, many people realized at the time that these areas of life were being secularized.

The best single example involves the medieval church's property. At the zenith of her power, the church owned about half of all of the land of Germany, half of France, between a third and a quarter of Great Britain, and much of the rest of continental Europe. There arose some ambitious princes and barons who had military power at their disposal, like Henry VIII of Great Britain, who saw and desired the church's properties and moved to seize that property. They sacked the monasteries and reappropriated the church's lands to private or public use. When these properties were seized, it was said, even then, that the property was being "secularized," i.e., the church's control and influence was literally being withdrawn. These events kicked off the conscious beginning of the secularization process in western history. This process reached into and "liberated" other areas of life and thought.

Another well-documented example of the secularization of an area of life is in economics. Once, as R. H. Tawney demonstrated, the church believed that it was humanly impossible to serve both God and mammon.[6] So the medieval church set up a strong and conscious ethic of economics, that economic and business enterprises might serve higher purposes than man's greed. The church formulated the doctrine of the just price, to assure that cost approximated worth. They prohibited excessive interest, calling it usury—a sin for which one could go to hell. They established the guild system among the various crafts and vocations, to ensure the integrity of products and services.

Later, the West witnessed the rise of capitalism—which transformed the money-ethics relationship so radically that today no one pretends that the church significantly influences what happens in the economic realm. Indeed, it is becoming increasingly evident that there may be no effective ethical check upon man's economic greed, and greedy people and institutions now exhaust the earth's resources faster than the earth can replenish them.

Other areas of life which have been secularized with the fall of Christendom include the following:

1. Science
2. Literature
3. Education
4. Government
5. Art
6. Architecture
7. Community Life
8. Personal Morality
9. Holy Days and Seasons
10. Sunday

The reader who has not completely repressed his schooling in western history will remember the story of each of these areas of life that were once influenced by the church, but are now secularized.

The secularization process began in the fifteenth and sixteenth centuries. It accelerated in the nineteenth and twentieth centuries, stampeded by the Industrial Revolution and the rise of the modern city which dislocated peoples from their traditions. This process is in a fairly advanced stage in our time, with certain pockets of cultural lag.

It should not be assumed that secularization has taken precisely the same form in every culture in the West. As Martin Marty has suggested, Europe has experienced *utter* secularity—God and the church are attacked, while England has experienced mere secularity—God and the Church are being ignored in daily routine and public policy, and the U.S.A. has experienced controlled secularity or American Civil Religion—in which the symbols of Christianity have been maintained, but now carry the freight of pagan meanings and are used for non-Christian ends.[7]

This whole story is significant for evangelism because it was in Christendom that the church became a great, powerful, and central institution, and every person in the culture automatically understood himself to be Christian. Today, this advantageous situation no longer exists. And since few in the church really perceive our new missionary setting in the West, Christian evangelists are speaking to a world that no longer exists, except in nostalgia and in pockets of cultural lag.

GENERALIZATIONS ABOUT SECULAR PEOPLE

How have people changed because of the secularization process?

Most basically (and obviously), great numbers of people now can live their lives and make their decisions without conscious regard to the Christian faith, the Christian church, or Christian parsons if they want to. This is secularization of influence. People are now influenced by many religions, philosophies, life-styles, and assumptions, not just by Christianity.

We have observed a post-Christendom secularization of vocabulary. Most people do not know the meaning (or even the referent) for the most basic Christian terms. For instance, how many people in our church could satisfactorily define Justification? Sin? Kingdom of God? Faith? Love?

We have also observed a secularization of human consciousness. In the Middle Ages, people spent much time thinking about God, Christian doctrines, saints, Holy Days, and angels. They lived their lives in terms of the Christian calendar, the Christian seasons, etc. Today the consciousness of the average human being is not "stacked" in Christianity's favor. The American consciousness is filled with much data from entertainment, television, film, magazines, and other secular enterprises that are not derived from the Christian faith.

There is one thing that has not changed about secular people: People are still "religious beings." "Secular" and "religious" are not mutually exclusive terms. To become secular does not mean to become unreligious or devoid of some kind of religion. The awareness of transcendence and the search for the ultimate have not been wiped out of modern consciousness by the secularization process. Secularization theologians (excepting a few mavericks) usually stress only that the Church no longer writes everybody's religious agenda. People remain religious beings, but they are religious in many different ways in our increasingly secular and pluralistic culture. As Dean Kelley, in *Why Conservative Churches Are Growing,* has reminded us—people need religion.[8] People are intrinsically religious beings. They need some religion that presumes "to explain the meaning of life in ultimate terms." Every person wants his life and history to make sense. Furthermore, people do yearn to contact and be right with whatever it is that is ultimate. They sense that the human quests for self-understanding and justification are dependent upon being right with Reality.

In our post-Christendom era and secular setting, the church is no longer the only religious option open to people. They now reach out, in increasing numbers, in many religious and quasi-religious directions from astrology to civil religion, to witchcraft, to Zen Buddhism, to the Moonie cult. For example, one study showed that between forty and fifty million people per day in this country read their horoscope. We cannot know for sure how many take it seriously, but nevertheless that ancient approach to ultimacy is enjoying a resurgence in our lifetime. There is extensive interest in the occult, as demonstrated by the unprecedented popularity of *The Exorcist,* and in other forms of the quest for transcendence and mystery, e.g., *Close Encounters of the Third Kind.* Our generation has witnessed the rise of new kinds of religions, parareligions, and even strange religions. People worship just about anything these days. A fifteen-year-old Mahariji Guru almost filled the Houston Astrodome. He proclaimed to be personally ushering in a new era of peace, and it seems that most of the people who attended took him seriously.

Man's continuing religious quest for meaning and righteousness with ultimacy is especially obvious in the great political and economic "isms" that have cropped up in the nineteenth and twentieth centuries—Facism, Nazism, Communism, Capitalism, Nationalism, Imperialism, Racism. These varied "isms" have one factor in common: each of their followers assume that their particular "ism" has transcendent backing. Whatever the ultimate force of the universe is believed to be (Marxism's dialectical process, capitalism's free market mechanism, imperialism's "manifest destiny," Nazism's Aryan supremacy, etc.), they assume that the ultimate force of the universe is on their side and is behind their cause. Therefore, their cause is regarded as holy, and they demand devout commitment from their followers.

So, in a secular age where the church no longer controls or automatically influences people and institutions, people are still religious in the basic sense that they still look to and rely upon alleged supernatural or supramundane realities or powers to complete themselves. Like Linus' blanket, men still confer power upon external objects to make themselves feel secure, to bring them hope. These objects are idols, but their worship demonstrates that people still want cosmic backing for what they are and for what they do. So, it cannot be demonstrated that secular man is unreligious, but what can be said about him?

Five generalizations seem both defensible and worth emphasis. All five were originally delineated by a single great Christian apologist, Great Britain's Donald Lord Soper. Soper, now in his mid-seventies, is no mere desk academician, speculating about some abstract "modern man." Rather, Soper is the one man who has accepted the challenge to communicate the gospel and its causes to resistant secular people more seriously and continuously than anyone else in the twentieth century. Consequently, he has been more in contact with secular resistant non-Christians than anyone else in the English-speaking world.

Donald Soper, now Lord Soper, has served in Great Britain's House of Lords since 1963 and is a leading advocate for the "Bevanite wing" of the Labour Party.

He is also a radio and television personality in Great Britain, seen and heard on the BBC almost weekly for many years. But Donald Soper's real forum is not his pulpit at Kingsway Hall in London, nor the House of Lords, nor the BBC, so much as it is the open air.

More than fifty years ago, a young man from his congregation ventured to hear the speakers at Tower Hill—a setting for open air oratory since 1646. The speakers commend from soap boxes or atop a wall their various causes and ideologies. Some attract hundreds of interested auditors; others attract only disinterested pigeons. This young spectator saw that the Christians were faring rather badly in competition with the Marxists, the Militarists, and the other advocates. He mentioned this fiasco to Donald Soper, then a young minister in a church in London, who had been an accomplished debater at Cambridge. Soper immediately decided to visit Tower Hill the next Wednesday and defend the embattled faith. Years later, he acknowledged, "Had I known as much of the Hill as I do now I should probably not have agreed so glibly to put matters right." But Soper did go, and he has continued this weekly ministry of advocacy for some fifty years!

Every Wednesday, from atop an elevated rostrum, he faces as many people as can get within earshot, to advocate the gospel and its causes in the context of question and answer, challenge and response. He summarizes his contribution to the day's controversy and issues an appeal in the last few minutes of the hour and a half. In his fifty-year ministry at Tower Hill (and his forty-six years at Speaker's Corner, Hyde Park), he has received about fifty questions or challenges per meeting. From the extensive exposure to secular people, Soper confesses that "I do not pretend to know all the answers to the questions that men pose, but I do know all of the questions!''

Lord Soper has been in more intense contact with the mind, questions, and challenges of grassroots secular non-Christians than any other western Christian of our lifetime. When he speaks about secular people—who and where they are, what their questions are, and what their assumptions are—the church would do well to listen. Besides experience, he brings an awesome set of credentials to the task. A Ph.D. from London University, his dissertation was written about a phase of the secularization process in the cities of France, so that he approached this ministry with a lucid grasp of the history and nature of secularization. He has an encyclopedic mind and retains virtually everything that he reads and hears. His gifts in rhetoric and argument are formidable. There are few Marxists in the English-speaking world who will debate him publicly. He is the one modern Christian most prepared to generalize about secular people and to instruct us in ways to reach and engage them.

The basic Soper source on this topic are his now-classic 1960 Lyman Beecher Lectures at Yale Divinity School, published as *The Advocacy of the Gospel,* particularly chapter 1.[9] The five generalizations that follow, however, are not restricted to this seminal source.

FROM KNOWLEDGE TO IGNORANCE

According to Dr Soper, the first change in people caused by secularization that is important for evangelical communication is one from basic knowledge to fundamental ignorance about Christian matters. Back in

Christendom, even common illiterate people knew a great deal about Christianity. They had been schooled in the catechism. They lived their lives in terms of the church year.[10]

Today, people simply do not know nearly as much about basic Christian matters. Because of the secularization of areas of life that once assured the transmission of Christian ideas—education, publishing, Christian year, etc.—most people are now quite ignorant of basic Christian matters. When Gallup surveyed the American people in 1950, and asked them to name the four Gospels, he found that fifty-three out of every hundred Americans could not name even one of the Gospels! Not only are masses of people ignorant about basic Christianity, many are basically misinformed. They identify Christianity with being a nice person or abstention from drinking or good citizenship.

FROM DEATH TO LIFE

The second change in persons caused by secularization is one of degree—change in consciousness from a death-orientation to a life-orientation. In Christendom, death was not camouflaged by sophisticated morticians. The corpse stayed in the home until the day of the funeral. People lived cheek by jowl with death. Before the ascent of medical science, history knew plagues, epidemics, pestilences, and famines, in which half of a population could be wiped out in a year or two. Every time you got sick, you knew that the illness could snowball and finish you. Until fairly recent times, life expectancy was about thirty-five. So for understandable reasons throughout most of history people have been preoccupied with death, and their questions have been concerned with the survival of personal identity and consciousness beyond death. For centuries, more thinking, more writing, more questions were raised about death than any other single subject.

For us, the situation vis à vis death is significantly different. Today, morticians camouflage the reality of death—lessening our reflection about death. Our life expectancy is more than double what it has been throughout most of recorded history. Through inoculation and immunization, epidemics are fairly well in check. When you get sick today, it is not usually a crisis, but an inconvenience. So today, people are significantly less death-oriented and more life-oriented. To a greater degree people are now asking questions like, How do you cope in this life? How do you make sense out of this life? How do you get along with people? How do you find meaning and purpose?

FROM GUILT TO DOUBT

Third, and most important according to Soper, is the shift from guilt to doubt as the number one factor in the evangelist's audience. A couple of decades ago, Soper was visiting with Dr. J. Earnest Ratenbury who had been a leader of British Methodism for a quarter of a century. Soper asked, "What changes have you noticed in congregations since you began preaching sixty-five years ago?" Ratenbury answered, "In any congregation sixty-five years ago you could count on a general sense of guilt. Now the only thing you can count on is a general sense of doubt!"[11]

Soper says that although guilt was once the major

problem of a preacher's audince, today doubt is the major problem in his audience's consciousness. This does not mean that people are not guilty anymore, nor that guilt does not continue to be a real and conscious problem for people. Indeed, Soper observes that a general sense of guilt remains. But much of the remaining sense of guilt is now either projected or explained away. For example, guilt is projected when people acknowledge guilt-induced problems, but they claim that "it is not my guilt, it is the establishment (or the youth or the Communists or someone else) who is guilty." Or, in some cases, guilt is explained away. We see modern people going to therapists with their guilt feelings, not seeking forgiveness for their guilt, but freedom from their guilt feelings. Soper suggests that "the profound sense of personal guilt has almost disappeared."[12] But the main point he makes is that "doubt has taken the place of guilt as the common factor in the constitution of the preacher's crown." He believes that one day this era will be named "the age of dubiety."

Now, what is the significance of doubt in evangelical communication? Soper suggests that: "Guilt is like tinder that blazes when the spark of emotion is applied to it; whereas doubt is like a rust which can only be removed by careful polishing."[13] Soper means that if you have the luxury of speaking to people who now want forgiveness, you will find this to be a relatively easy communication task because their response will come fairly readily. But, if you are speaking to people whose major obstacle to faith is doubt, you will find evangelizing them a more difficult and protracted process. The advocate must be content to chip away over time rather than to unrealistically rely upon a single transaction. So, as Soper admonishes, "We must begin where people are, rather than where we would like them to be; and we must not ask too much of them too soon."

FROM NEED TO CURIOSITY

The fourth change in persons caused by secularity is a shift from a sense of need for Christianity to a sense of curiosity about Christianity and Christians. Once, virtually all people knew of their religious need and believed Christianity could meet the need. In frontier America, for instance, even the town reprobate knew that he needed salvation. Today, secular people do not generally perceive the nature of their need, and although they search they do not perceive that what they really need is something that Christianity offers. Human beings in the twentieth century are not complete and without needs. The missing link is one of perception in regard to the relevance of the Christian faith for meeting the deepest needs of our beings. Soper would say, ask the man in the street what Christianity is basically about, and he will reply: "Well, Christianity has to do with rituals and moral goodness and good citizenship. Christianity is preoccupied with ecclesiastical affairs, ecumenical meetings, and petty doctrinal squabbles." The man in the street will acknowledge, however, that "Christianity is OK, especially for little children and for adults who like that kind of thing." The supreme tragedy is that the average person does not even perceive that the hopes and fears of all of his years are met in Jesus Christ. People are not aware that their needs are intrinsically related to what Christianity has to offer. Instead, they are curious, increasingly curious about what Christians believe and why they believe it. They especially wonder about Christian credibility—"Do Christians really live by what they believe? And does it make any real difference in their lives? Could Christianity change the world?"

FROM BELONGING TO ALIENATION

Fifth, back in Christendom people felt like they belonged to a greater degree.[14] They felt at home in their world. Today people feel alienated. They feel estranged. This is partly due to their submersion in a secular technopolis. A century ago, Ralph Waldo Emerson confessed, "I always feel some loss of faith upon entering cities; they are great conspiracies." Soper contends that people have been alienated in three of their major relationships as a consequence of secular urbanizations.

First, urban people are alienated from nature. They have been estranged or separated from the soil, from the rhythms of life, and from their fellow nonhuman creatures. Once, men were in intimate contact with the awe and beauty of nature, receiving whatever hints or clues about the ultimate that nature had to share. But now since people are separated from nature and herded into cities they do not perceive these hints or clues. Theodore Wickham, a Bishop of the Church of England, writes, "There is no more lethal foe of natural religion than the artificiality of industrialized civilization." William Blake, a nineteenth century poet and mystic, expressed the urban eclipse of natural revelation in these memorable words: "Great things happen when men and mountains meet, but these things do not happen when men jostle in the street."

Second, people in mass urban society feel alienated from the sources of political power. Soper observes that the man in the street "is alienated because he feels he has no lot or part in the actual conduct of affairs." That is, most people today feel powerless. They feel they are victims of the decision makers in government and industry who do not listen to them, or who only pretend to listen. Many people doubt that the economic and political systems on which they depend are responsive to them, or even care about them.

Thirdly, the man in technopolis is alienated from his neighbors. In the city's gigantic high-rise apartments people live anonymously, generally not knowing the names of the other people on their floor. All of us have experienced an elevator ride to the top of a city skyscraper; people crowd into the elevator, and while it is ascending each person is looking at the dial and pretending that the other people do not exist. Soper exclaims: "The great cities . . . have become denatural-ized, so that there is no sense of community even at the level of tittle-tattle. There is no sense of community even at the level of being thrown too close together. There is no center to the life which people live. This is the supreme problem of the outsider."[15]

STRATEGIES FOR COMMUNICATING THE GOSPEL
TO RESISTANT SECULAR PEOPLE

The foregoing analysis raises many questions. How do you get the gospel across? How do you help people discover the rescuing and fulfilling possibility that God extends to them through Christ's church? Without any desire to be either exotic or original, several principles are supremely important in communicating to secular people. I turn first to elements of strategy, and then to especially relevant facets of the gospel.

First, because secular people are largely ignorant rather than knowledgeable about basic Christian matters, one essential element of the church's strategy must be instruction. Soper stresses that instruction to outsiders must "begin at the beginning" with the basics of Christianity, "rather than beginning at the middle."[16] What is Christianity basically about? What was Jesus Christ teaching? What did the Apostles claim about him? What is the heart of the call that he extends to human beings? What are the basics? These are precisely the things that the secular person does not know. Soper believes that church communicators avoid the usual mistake of presupposing a knowledge (and vocabulary) that people do not in fact possess. In one of his earliest books Donald Soper pleaded for "the patient explanation, over and over again, to the ordinary man and woman of what the Christian faith really is and what it offers; not what they take it to be. Only then can the appeal for personal surrender be honorably made."

The second element of strategy engages the fact of widespread religious doubt. The appropriate strategy, as suggested by Soper's open-air advocacy using question and response, calls for stress on dialogue—or sharing the gospel within dialogue. In an age of doubt we must engage doubting people at the point of their conscious doubts. We do them no service if we skirt their doubts or dodge their doubts or pretend that their doubts do not exist. You only help doubting people by engaging their doubts, bringing them to the surface, and ventilating them. This can be done in preaching by raising questions rhetorically and then addressing them, although this is best done in conversation. But whatever the format, when we engage people's doubts, we sometimes answer and resolve some of them, and we help a person live with those that cannot, for now, be satisfactorily answered or resolved.

Third, since many secular people are curious about Christians and unacquainted with basic Christianity, we have the opportunity, through a necessarily subtle strategy, to demonstrate the credibility of Christian people. That is, if people are wondering not only what we believe, but whether we really live by it and whether it makes any difference, then we are obliged to demonstrate how it does make an authentic difference. Stephen Neill, the great missiologist, writes that the initial factor in the conversion of many non-Christians was their perception of "some action on the part of a Christian which presented itself as radically different from the kind of action which would have been taken by a non-Christian in similar circumstances."[17] Non-Christians must see that Christians live by resources that are not generally available to, or at least appropriated by, most people. This suggestion does not mean that we should flaunt our credentials or wear our sacrifices on our sleeves or indulge in unrequested spiritual autobiography. The demonstration of our credibility must be subtle and indirect—as a by-product of whatever we're doing. But those people to whom we would communicate do have the right to see that we are gripped and changed and guided by the faith that we commend to them, and that we are giving our life to the faith's causes.[18]

The fourth element of strategy takes seriously the fact that secular people do not perceive the relevance of Christianity to their needs and motives. The appropriate strategy is to speak promptly and explicitly to the basic human needs and motives that grip and dominate people in our time. People have needs, just as they've always had needs, though they may not be dominated by precisely the same needs, wants, and motives as were their ancestors. They are higher on Maslow's hierarchy of human motivation. The difference is not that they no longer have needs, but that they no longer perceive the relevance of Christianity to meet those needs. Soper's open-air strategy is to begin by speaking to some human problem or to some human need or to some crisis that has many people in its clutches. This principle is even more easily implemented in conversational one-to-one evangelism where we first listen to discern where a person is hurting or searching, and then share a relevant facet of the gospel. What do people need? It might be a need for self-acceptance, or their suffering, emptiness, or boredom. It might be a search for purpose, need for fellowship or love, or the need to count for something. If Maslow doesn't turn us on, we are constrained to make our own classifications based on observations of who people are, what they are searching for, wanting and needing. Soper's point is that we must first demonstrate the relevance of our gospel by beginning where people are in their conscious needs and motives. Having demonstrated the relevance of what we are about to share, thereby winning their attention, we then plug in the facet of the gospel that is relevant good news for the need or motive that has been engaged.

As a fifth strategy, since people today are alienated from their neighbors, we need to provide that Christian resource we call koinonia. Virtually all human beings need fellowship. No man is an island. He needs to be known, affirmed, loved, esteemed, and to belong in a community. These are intrinsic human needs, and people are not truly human apart from fellowship. This is why we need never feel squeamish about inviting people into membership in a Christian congregation. People need to be "members one of another." This was a primary appeal of the apostolic church in all of the mediterranean world. "See how those Christians love one another?" is rightfully a primary appeal of today's church. The koinonia group is here to stay. Push it. People yearn for the fellowship that only Christian koinonia can offer.

RELEVANT FACETS OF THE MESSAGE

There are also facets of the Christian message that seem especially "right" for secular people. We have every right to be confident that there are facets of our message that have the power to grip many secular people immediately. I will mention three.

First, in view of the fact that people are less death-oriented and more life-oriented and are asking, "How can we discover the meaning of the human pilgrimage and our purpose in this life?" we commend this message: In Christ and his mission through the church you can find your meaning! Christ is the clue. Following him leads to meaning. Many college students and young urban adults, hungering for a satisfying worldview or to make sense of their personal lives, are finding that this message speaks to them.

Second, since people today are alienated we need not only provide the reality of fellowship, but also proclaim to them the message: "You are known and loved." God knows you so intimately that "the hairs on your head are numbered." As St. Augustine put it, "He loves each one of us as if there was only one of us to love."

People need to hear that. A well-known Christian writer told a story about his wife and her volunteer work in a mental hospital for emotionally disturbed children. There was a little black boy whom she had especially grown to love. He had never known his mom and dad. He had been relayed from one relative to another; now by age of eight, he was schizophrenic. One day he asked her, "Do you suppose that there's anybody in the world who loves me?" She said, "Why Jimmy, I love you, I love you very much." He asked her, somewhat unexpectedly, "Do you suppose God loves me?" She said, "I'm sure he does, I know he does, and I'll tell you what, I'll send the chaplain around so that he can explain God's love for you." And the little boy said, "Oh, I'd like that." Several days later when she returned for another volunteer day at the hospital she found the little boy crouched over in his corner, seemingly more withdrawn than before. Surprised, she asked him, "Did the chaplain come to talk to you about how God loves you?" The little boy snapped back, "Don't talk to me about him!" She asked, "Why, didn't he come talk to you?" He replied, "Yes, but all he did was ask me to sing in the choir!" The point is crucial: If all we can offer to people is the opportunity to do our ecclesiastical chores, we had better not bother. If we withhold from people the Bread of life for which they hunger, we betray our calling. People must know that they are loved, unconditionally loved, deeply loved, in the very core of their being from the heart of the universe.

Third, since people are alienated from their world and the sources of power, we must proclaim Christian causes and call them to work for those causes. Here, evangelism becomes the handmaid to mission, or to the expression of mission we call social action. We must proclaim to people that "there are Christian causes to which you can give your life, causes that are of the essence of the kingdom of God, and if you'll give your life to those causes you can make a difference." Lord Soper once dramatized this appeal in an article responding to Archbishop Temple's project, "Toward the Conversion of England":

I want men to know that by giving their allegiance to Christianity they will be embarking upon a great campaign to banish war and poverty and injustice, to overthrow the false and corrosive doctrines of State, Empire and race purity, and to set up a communal life where love and service have taken the place of selfishness and armed might. But, just as important, I want the church which sends out this manifesto to be the advance copy of that new world it preaches.[19]

In another statement Donald Soper speaks of the kind of evangelist who can effectively commend his message:

The credentials of an evangelist are his experience of God as a Father and his vision and programme for a new world; if these are his, he must become a missionary.[20]

CHAPTER V

THE GRAND STRATEGY: DISCOVER RECEPTIVE PEOPLE

The Church Growth movement's greatest contribution to this generation's world evangelization will be its stress upon *receptivity*. The church is called to discover, reach, and disciple receptive people—i.e., people who are *now* ready and open to really consider the Christian possibility for their lives. Because of extensive historical and cultural research, much more is now known about what causes receptivity in people and how receptive people can be identified than has ever been known before. Congregations and denominations will find, in the principles and strategies of receptivity, a gold mine of possibilities.

The strategy of focusing on receptive people has significant biblical warrant and is elaborated much more by writers like Donald McGavran and Peter Wagner than I will do here.[1] The missionary movement recorded in the New Testament believed that God prepares certain "harvests" of peoples, and he wants to send out his missionary laborers to gather those harvests (Lk. 10:2).

Some populations are analogous to the "good soil" which, when the seed of God's Word is planted in it, will take root, grow, and multiply. We must let those people hear the gospel who have ears to hear (Mk. 4:9). Jesus admonished those being sent out to "shake the dust" of resistant towns off their feet and hurry on to the next town which might be more receptive to the message of the inbreaking reign of God (Lk. 9:5).

Many passages in the Book of Acts reflect this strategy in action. For instance, the initial target population that Paul typically engages in a new town or city is the "godfearers"—the Gentile fellow-travelers of the synagogues who were attracted to the religion of the Jews, but unwilling to become Jews culturally. When one of the apostles preaches the new Faith that is both continuous with Judaism and also its fulfillment, but which allows Gentiles to keep their own culture, he finds these prepared people very receptive. So consciously and strategically he begins with this most receptive target audience in each city. This principle has been demonstrated in hundreds of populations and mission fields throughout the centuries. Today, it emerges as a more explicit strategy than it has been in quite some time.

Why does this strategy work? Or rather, when people become receptive, why do they? There is much mystery in the phenomenon of one person (or people) being receptive, another interested, another indifferent, another resistant, and still another hostile. Christian theology does not even pretend to have satisfactorily explained this. This is an ultimate and largely unprobed mystery about human beings. The Calvinist doctrine that some people are simply elected by God for salvation (and some are not) represents one historic attempt to take this mystery seriously.

A twofold explanation will give the evangelizing congregation enough knowledge to form a basis for action. First, some events and circumstances in the life of a person (or a people) open doors that stimulate an openness to new life-possibilities and permit the reception of previously screened-out messages. Second, God's Holy Spirit works through the events and circumstances of some people's lives to create receptivity, to "warm the heart" for the gospel. This is the Wesleyan doctrine of prevenient grace. Our gracious God goes before us into the hearts and consciousness of people, preparing for an evangelical harvest, which then takes place as he makes his actual appeal through us, his ambassadors (II Cor. 5:20). So, the Church's major strategy is to find those whom the Father is drawing to himself (John 6:44). Arthur Glasser explains that

there is a time when God's Spirit is peculiarly active in the hearts of men. They become "ripe unto harvest." As a result, all evangelistic activity should be in response to an awareness of where God is at work. Down through the years, as a result of a great deal of "soil testing" and field research, we have found that wherever this empirical factor has been deliberately made determinative of strategy, God has abundantly confirmed with good harvests. Indeed we feel we have leaped over the inscrutable mystery that down through the years has provoked endless theological debate and ecclesiastical division, and have put strength where it furthers, not hinders, the ongoing of the Christian mission. In seeking to win those whom God has made winnable we have not unnaturally gained new insight into what it means to be co-laborers with God in the building of His Church.[2]

A NEW MOTIVATION FOR URGENCY

In the teaching of the Church Growth movement, the new motivation for evangelistic urgency comes from the fact that people who are receptive and winnable today may not be tomorrow—or at least, next year. Donald McGavran sees the world (and each society) as a "mosaic" of people with their own particular cultures and subcultures. At any given time, some "pieces" of the colored mosaic are receptive (or "warm") to the gospel, others are resistant (or "cool"), and others are at various degrees in between. This colorful mosaic is complicated by the fact that the pieces do not remain the same color indefinitely. The relative receptivity of each subculture (and each person) fluctuates. McGavran contends, on the basis of extensive research in many cultures over forty-plus years, that

the receptivity or responsiveness of individuals waxes and wanes. No person is equally ready at all times to follow "The Way." . . . Peoples and societies also vary in responsiveness. Whole segments of mankind resist the gospel for periods—often very long periods—and then ripen to the Good News.

McGavran warns that receptivity wanes as often as it waxes. Like the tide, it comes in and goes out. Unlike the tide, no one can guarantee when it goes out that it will soon come back again.[3]

That fact of fluctuating receptivity should be a cause for the missionary congregation's evangelistic urgency. The Church must find and win winnable people while they are winnable. The history of missions is strewn with cosmic embarrassments—cases of peoples who were ripe for God's harvest, but whom the church ignored until receptivity had diminished, new resistance had set in, and it was too late to reap God's harvest. The strategic congregation is called, in each season, to discern and reach those who, for now, are receptive. The church that so cooperates with the prevenient grace of the Lord of the harvest will be a growing church with contagious power.

INDIGENOUS METHODS FOR RECEPTIVE PEOPLE

It is possible, however, to be amidst a receptive people and not reap the harvest that the Spirit has prepared. This is the case for the same reason that one might enter a ripe wheat field with a corn picker and not in fact be able to gather the wheat into the barn. Despite our timeliness and good intentions, if the method we use does not fit the particular harvest, we will be ineffective. In evangelism too, our approach and method must fit the target harvest. McGavran declares that "no single method will fit all populations."[4] Part of our task is to discover or fashion an approach that is indigenous to the particular person or group.

Expanding Jesus' fishers of men metaphor, McGavran and Win Arn show why "in great measure, responsiveness is related to approach."[5] At a given time, a certain species of fish may be responsive to one particular bait, but not to another, or may be interested by one type of fishing (say, fly casting), but not by another (plug casting).

> The good fisherman continues to seek responsiveness until he discovers the right bait for a particular fish during a particular season. He knows when he has the right bait—he's catching fish. As fish respond to one approach and not to another, so do people.[6]

And likewise, we know when we are employing the right outreach approach for a particular subculture when significant numbers are responding to the gospel in faith and are becoming disciples of Jesus Christ and responsible members of his church.

Mind you, no approach can win very resistant people while they are resistant. And, almost any culturally appropriate approach can harvest very receptive people. But for people somewhere in between strong resistance and strong receptivity, the use of the most indigenous and effective strategy possible is all-important. Because approach and method are such important variables, no congregation should glibly or prematurely give up on people until all attempts at inventing an indigenous method have been exhausted.[7]

What factors inform our discovery of approaches and methods that enable fairly receptive people to respond? McGavran and Arn, in stressing that fairly receptive people will respond to some approaches (but not others), comment on one factor as follows:

This is the truth behind the common opinion that a friendly church is a growing church. It is a matter of response. If a church is friendly, genuinely interested in people, and meeting their needs, it will find people responsive. They will be open to the Good News. On the other hand, if a Church is cold and reserved, that Church will probably find people in its ministry area cold and indifferent.[8]

Let's list, somewhat systematically, several more factors that help inform the "right approach" for the population you have targeted.

1. The people of the church are friendly toward those receptive people, not merely friendly in general, but genuinely and specifically interested in them and affirming of them.

2. The church effectively assimilates receptive persons into its worship, group life, ministries, and leadership.
3. The preaching, witnessing, and teaching of the church "speaks their language" so that they discover revelation coming through the words—they really understand and sense that the faith is good news for them, not an alien propaganda.
4. The message and ministries of the church engage their strongest motives and felt needs.
5. The church and its ministries "fit" the prospects culturally. There is an absence of class intimidation or cultural imperialism. The target people subjectively and spontaneously resonate with the Church's music, architecture, hymnody, and worship and preaching style.
6. *Who* reaches out to prospective Christians is an important factor. (a) If the witnesser is a person within their intimate social network (a relative, friend, colleague, etc.) who is a transparently credible Christian and has some influence with them, then the chances of positive response are generally the greatest. (b) If the witnesser comes from outside their social network but is a member of their "homogeneous unit,"[9] the chances of positive response are next greatest. (c) If the witnesser is an especially credible Christian, is gifted in cross-cultural communication, appears to love them, wants the best for them, is willing to take risks to reach them, and is willing to contact the same person a number of times—then positive response to the messenger and the Message is also possible from many receptive persons in a target population—but probably not all. In a new target population the first messenger will frequently be an outsider (c), but the movement of witness will

move to (b) and especially to (a) as rapidly as possible.

7. The congregation should reach out to individuals in proportion to their relative receptivity on the resistency-receptivity continuum. That is, the more receptivity they now reveal, the more often one would visit them.

THE POLICY FOR RESISTANT PEOPLE

Parenthetically, I must add that in our emphasis upon reaching receptive people we must not abandon or "write off" people who, for now, are resistant (see the previous chapter). While strategic mission will send disproportionate numbers of witnessers to receptive people, some Christians will be placed within resistant pieces of the mosaic—especially Christians with special gifts, such as: strong inner faith, little need for multiple "victories" to keep incentive going, ability to love without immediate reward or returned love, sensitivity to where people are, good sense of timing, patience, and a deep conviction that people are worth spending one's life for.

A ministry among resistant peoples will mainly be one of presence, service, seed sowing—saying what is possible in a given situation without repelling people. McGavran counsels us to "occupy fields of low receptivity lightly." We should never appear to swamp or badger resistant people with too many witnessers or too much preaching—which would only drive them further away and make rigid their already hard hearts.[10]

Such strategy for resistant people is intrinsically valid, and our very presence may help cause their greater receptivity in measurable time. Our loving service among them may turn out to be one circumstance in their life and setting through which God's prevenient grace works to warm their hearts. For many peoples, this period will prove to be a very necessary season of plowing, seed sowing, cultivating, and watering in order to enable that harvest which will come to fruition in God's own time. Besides, we must have some presence among them so that when they do turn more receptive we shall perceive this and then send more laborers into the ripening field. Having no advocates among a resistant people is to risk our missing the time of their visitation.

INTRODUCING INDICATORS

This background raises what is perhaps the supreme question of evangelization strategy: "How do we discover receptive people, while they are receptive? The answer of all Church Growth researchers and strategists can be summarized in one word: *indicators.* An indicator is a phenomenon that is frequently found in a people's setting, history, or experience during and/or shortly before they turn to the Faith. For instance, (to use a ludicrous example) if most people become left-handed before turning toward the Christian possibility—that would be an indicator. A strategic church would be on the lookout for homogeneous populations in the process of becoming left-handed and would then saturate that population with missionaries. Notice, it does not especially matter whether the indicating phenomenon causes the receptivity or whether both the phenomenon and the receptivity have a common (but perhaps unknown) cause. That the phenomenon is frequently to be observed before or during actual receptivity is enough to serve as a useful indicator for locating receptive people.

We can discover many indicators by examining the history of evangelism, and if any past awakenings among many peoples were accompanied by a certain phenomenon, then when we perceive this phenomenon among a people today, we may reasonably guess that they are ready for a turning to the faith. Naturally, many indicators are "soft," and any strategy based upon using them cannot pretend to be foolproof. But, where several indicators are observed in the same population, the probability of actual receptivity being there increases. In any case, no strategic congregation should rely only on indicators to identify a target population for top priority saturation outreach. The church should "test the soil" by sending some surveyors or actual witnessers to make an adequate inquiry into the population's responsiveness. The indicators tell us where to test the soil.

GENERAL INDICATORS

The literature of Church Growth and Missionary Anthropology gives us several broad indicators that are helpful to begin with.

1. *Dissatisfaction:* People are frequently open to the Christian possibility when they are deeply dissatisfied with themselves and their lives. They are at a turning point when their needs are not being met and their motives are not being fulfilled by their current methods of coping. Consciously or subconsciously, they desire something new that will satisfy their needs or motives.[11]

2. *Cultural Change:* When significant elements of a culture are changing, this indicates weakened cultural

foundations or goals, and a search for new ones. Examples would include: changes in marriage and family patterns or values, changes in kinship structures and patterns, political change, economic change and changes in speech or language patterns. Edward Pentecost reports that "if Christianity is presented as the answer to the felt needs of economic, social, and political unrest and dissatisfaction, then it may receive a hearing at that level."[12] Pentecost does caution that in settings of culture change, Christianity must be presented and perceived by the people not as the destroyer, but the fulfiller of their culture. When people are experiencing cultural change, the amount of personal change will vary with individuals. Wagner recommends that "those who change their life-style most radically will be the ones approached first with the gospel . . . those who cling to their former ways will come lower on the priority scale."[13]

3. *Individual Stress:* Persons experiencing stress, especially increasing stress, will increasingly look for new ways to cope with or reduce that stress to a tolerable level. The kinds of symptoms people reveal under stress depend on their personality type. Flexible persons may be seen experimenting with various options. Regressive persons display such symptoms as alcoholism, extreme passivity, intragroup violence, disregard for kinship and sexual mores, or forms of depression and self-reproach.[14]

4. *The Masses:* In general, the church will usually find "the masses" to be more responsive then "the classes." Missionary strategy has often been very wrong in emphasizing outreach first to the classes and only later to the masses.[15]

5. *Growing Religions:* Roy Shearer points out that probably the only reasonably perfect indicator is the existence of an already growing religious body in the

target population. Obviously, "wherever we see a growing non-Christian religion, we can be sure the people in that place are potential receptors of the Gospel."[16] Christians should not presuppose that a growing non-Christian religion is actually fulfilling peoples' needs—it may only be engaging their needs in ways that will later prove unfulfilling—analogous to a thirsty man's drinking salty ocean water and engaging his thirst but not satisfying it. Christians should know instead that a growing religion or ideology indicates receptivity and therefore the call of the Lord of the harvest to his church. The time is ripe to move in and make Christian discipleship a live option for the searching people.

THIRD WORLD INDICATORS

Some more particularized indicators have been observed in the populations of Africa, Asia, and Latin America, which constitute the Third World. These indicators are not without relevance to North America's mission field, and are especially relevant to immigrant peoples and ethnic minorities who have Third-World linkages. Several representative indicators follow.

1. *New Settlements* Settlements of newly moved-in populations typically contain many receptive persons. This is especially the case when people have recently left their former clan and friends. They are now separated from the old pressures to conform and are free to make new friends, explore new possibilities, entertain new ideas. McGavran's research shows that many "are in a phase of insecurity, capable of reaching out for what will stabilize them and raise their spirits."[17] The Church should saturate such populations with missionaries to

evangelize and plant new congregations. But Wagner reports that "entire ethnic units which migrate to a new area for colonization but which retain their traditional language and customs will not usually be fruitful unless reached by evangelists from their own culture."[18]

2. *Conquest or Oppression* People are still being conquered in many parts of the world. This experience has a shattering effect upon the entire culture of the conquered. "Their pride is humbled, their values trampled underfoot, their institutions abolished, and their gods dethroned."[19] Frequently, conquered people will be very receptive to the gospel—especially if it is presented by someone not identified with the conquerors.

3. *The Removal of Oppression* Wagner reports that "when a people are oppressed for an extended period of time and do not enjoy liberty of thought and action, they often become highly receptive to the gospel when the oppression is finally removed."[20] This principle applies to the lifting of many kinds of controls on the action and behavior of people—such as release from the pressure to conform in family, class, or ethnic groupings or release from the government's former restrictions of freedom of conscience or religious freedom or release from the power of the society to ostracize deviants.

4. *Other Kinds of Political Change* Many other kinds of political change also induce receptivity among people. For instance, a country in the midst of a political revolution usually has responsive people.[21] Likewise, a wave of nationalism *may* aid the growth of the Church. Responsiveness under such conditions should be perceived as temporary; therefore, these receptive people must be reached quickly.

5. *Social and Economic Change* Peter Wagner explains that

whenever people are undergoing rapid or radical social and economic change, churches are likely to grow. People who are uprooted from familiar social surroundings and located in new ones find themselves searching for a new orientation to their lives. They are disposed to listen to the gospel, and many of them will recognize that Christ can become the integrating factor they need in their personal lives and in their community.

He adds that "Areas of rapid urbanization almost invariably contain large segments of population receptive to the gospel."[22]

GUIDELINES FOR DISCOVERING
RECEPTIVE MAINLINE AMERICANS

Many of the indicators of receptivity mentioned above—discovered primarily in research of growing churches and Christian movements in the Third Word—are relevant to America too, or to some of the subcultural pieces of America's population mosaic. As in other mission fields, our strategy for evangelizing this one should be informed by available indicators of receptive people. What follows are ten indicators, expressed as guidelines, which are especially relevant to much of America's mission field. Some of these indicators are from American Church Growth research, others from Third World research—but are saved for now or repeated now because of their special potency for the Christian mission to America.

1. *Pray to be led to receptive people.* God's Spirit works by his prevenient grace. Through certain events and circumstances, he is preparing people to hear the

gospel, to perceive his call to them, and to accept reconciliation with him and become followers of Christ. This same Spirit desires to lead us to those whom he is now preparing to meet him.

Therefore, pray to be so led. If you pray to be led to receptive people, you will "coincidentally" discover them—time and time again. Stop praying to be so led, and the "coincidences" will stop occurring! This is such a basic principle of missionary outreach that all of the other guidelines are its servants. We are not teaching a nonspiritual technology for evangelism. Indeed, such is not possible because evangelism is the Holy Spirit's work at every point: he prepares those whom he desires to call; he prepares and leads those whom he sends out; and if receptive people sense his approach through our outreach, and respond in faith—this too is his work.

2. *The people visiting and wanting to join your church are receptive people.* I begin with what must read like an excessively obvious indicator. I assure you that its obviousness cannot be assumed. In the year and a half prior to this writing, I have been in no less than seven congregations in which I happened to ask someone, "Are you a member of this family of Christ?" and the embarrassing reply has been (with some variation)— "No, I want to join. I've indicated this two or three times on the registration pad, but I've not heard from anybody. Say, how does a fellow join this church, anyway?" Yes, some congregations do not perceive the obviously receptive people.

Although visitors to our churches are very receptive people, their receptivity (at least to *that* church) is frequently short lived, and wanes rather quickly. Dr. Larry Lacour of the First United Methodist Church of Colorado Springs, Colorado has fashioned a strategy for reaching visitors. The first invitation to every visitor is to join a four-session orientation class—at the end of which it is hoped that each person will decide to profess faith in Christ and join the church. Joining the class is encouraged by three contacts—a phone call within twenty-four hours, a visit that week by the minister of evangelism, and a visit, also that week, by a team of lay people. Lacour reports that when they carry out this schedule some 90 percent join the class; if they are a week late, 50 percent join, if a month late, 10 percent.

3. *People who have recently lost faith (in anything) are very receptive.* Contemporary America is character-ized by religious anarchy. With so many options for religious and quasi-religious devotion, people are "into" everything from astrology to Zen, from Mormonism to Moonism, from drugs to the ancient superstitions of the Druids. These and many other religions and philosophies promise more than they deliver. A man places his confidence in one of them this year; that confidence erodes next year. McGavran explains that

Man is a believer by nature. If faith in old religion fades, he becomes responsive to some new religion—of science, communism, or an updated version of his ancestral cult. He may deify a new leader, his secular civilization, a political party, or Man—but worship he will. [23]

The missionary church should constantly be on the lookout for people "between idols." They constitute a receptive field of continuing harvest in most communi-ties.

4. *People among whom any church or religion is growing are receptive.* Because this is the one absolutely certain indicator, it deserves mention again. If any church, religion, or philosophy is growing among a

people, the Christian church should reach out to them and make Christian discipleship a meaningful option to them.

Do not presuppose that the non-Christian religion is actually fulfilling their needs—it may only be scratching where they itch. When the itch surfaces somewhere else, they will look elsewhere. Several weeks ago I was gently encountered by a pretty devotee of the Hare Krishna cult as she and several others were "working" a section of Chicago O'Hare airport. She began the conversation with the words—"Excuse me sir, but all of the handsome gentlemen are wearing carnations today. May I give you one?" She got my attention. We briefly conversed, and I remember saying: "Look, I know you're into this now—but it will leave you hollow and let down later. Whenever that happens, telephone me collect any time day or night." I gave her my card. She looked aside to be sure her partners were busy elsewhere; her eyes teared, and her voice trembled as she almost whispered— "Thank you, Mr. Hunter, I just might do that."

But what if the religion now growing among a population is another Christian church of your denomination, or another? The conventional wisdom of our generation, as influenced by ecumenism's policy of comity would contend that "we should stay out of their territory." Recently, this territorial understanding of one's parish has been challenged. If that church is in the midst of a harvest, the ministry of evangelization will need more laborers than one church can provide. No one church can fully reap a great harvest. It will have the indigenous methods, ministries, and style for reaching only some of the receptive people. The growing church will need the help of your church—whether they perceive it or not! If you move in and engage people they cannot win, both churches will prosper. Any crisis in interchurch relations will be temporary. In any case, fidelity to the Great Commission is even more important than static-free ecumenism. Wherever you find receptive searching people, you have no moral right to withhold from them the option of Christian discipleship through your congregation.

5. *People of the same homogeneous unit as your members will be more receptive to the outreach of your church.* Donald McGavran is famous for the assertion that "people like to become Christians without crossing significant linguistic, ethnic, or cultural barriers." People are more likely to respond to the appeal of a congregation whose members are perceived to be like them culturally, among whom they feel comfortable and accepted and with whom they can communicate easily.

Any community is composed of many H.U.s or groups of people who have some characteristic in common and who feel like they belong and can communicate because of that characteristic. The basis of this sense of homogeneous belonging may be common language or dialect, ethnicity, cultural background, socioeconomic class, vocational grouping, educational attainment—or some combination of these factors. The congregation must be sensitive to the social realities of its environment. Cultural anthropologists feel that "people conscious-ness" or "consciousness of kind" is very important to self-identity and social interaction in all societies.[24]

It has been found that every church grows more effectively among some groups of people than others—because its ministries are more indigenous to the subculture and felt needs of the particular people. Part of your strategy should be to analyze the active members of your present congregation. Into what homogeneous groups do they roughly cluster? When you have identified the H.U.s in your congregation, interview people from each group to determine which ministries of the congregation originally attracted them, and which ministries are meaningful and helpful to them now. Then find all the people in your ministry area who are like them and offer these people those same ministries and resources of your congregation and its expression of the gospel.

6. *People of the same homogeneous unit as visitors and new converts in your congregation will be very receptive to the outreach of your church.* This is a version of the previous principle, but it especially provides an up-to-date indicator of the contagious strengths of your congregation as well as the homogenous populations that would be most receptive to your congregation's appeal. This time, classify the dominant H.U.s of your visitors and new converts. Interview them, especially all of the new converts from over the past three years, to discover the ministries, the truths, and the ports of entry that are engaging them. Then discover and reach out to all such people in your entire ministry area and offer those ministries and faith-resources to them. As in all outreach, do not be content with the modest (at best) harvest you will reap from an initial contact. Even with receptive people, repeated contacts must be made. It is through the cumulative effect of repeated conversations that people work through the possibility and take steps of response toward discipleship.

7. *Identify people with conscious needs that your ministries can help.* The strategic church knows that an opening to most people is found in one of the dominant

life motives that write the conscious agenda in their lifelong quest for wholeness and fulfillment. The reason for this strategy is that people are attracted to the Christian faith when they perceive that Christianity is a better way to fulfill their needs than what they are currently depending on.

In a pattern similar to the one above, find people in the congregation whose needs are met by the life and ministries of your church. Identify the particular ministries and the needs they meet. Then find all the people with the same needs and offer them these proven ministries.

Use the people who are helped by your congregation's ministries in the program of outreach. For example, in one church, a group of divorced persons has found great help in the support strength of their small group—with lessons, sharing sessions, speakers, and prayers focused upon their felt needs. These group members make credible and contagious visits to other people who have experienced divorce, offering the group's ministry to the persons who need it.

8. *Identify target populations for whom you could begin new ministries.* Lyle Schaller's twenty years of research on growing congregations shows that most growing churches have a specialty in addition to their basic ministries.[25] These special ministries are fashioned to engage unreached target populations in the community. People at Robert Schuller's Garden Grove Community Church regularly canvass a neighborhood with a felt needs survey. When they find a cluster of people with a need that no one else is ministering to, Garden Grove begins a relevant new ministry for these people and then invites them to receive it. Schuller believes that "the secret of success is to find a need and fill it."

A Friends' church in Southern California identified in

their ministry area a large number of undiscipled young couples with small children. They launched a periodic "potty training seminar," a mother's-day-out program, new young couples' Sunday school classes, weekly home Bible studies for housewives, bowling teams, and opportunities for both wives and husbands to serve in the community—with a nursery always provided. This church reaped a harvest among young couples.

Another church discovered a large number of "mature adults," those fifty-five and older. They lessened their conspicuous family emphasis and launched ministries to individuals as individuals—a counseling program, opportunities to use nonverbal creative gifts for the church's work (such as making leper bandages for a colony in Liberia), amplified hospital and bereavement ministries and many daytime activities at the church.

Many churches are waking up to the fact that some 60 percent of the people in America have creative gifts that are other than cognitive or verbal in nature. Many people express their greatest gifts through their hands. One church in Saginaw, Michigan, has built an industrial arts complex on the second floor of the educational building called The Carpenter's Shop. They actively recruit men with "shop" interests. Dozens of men have joined the faith and that church through the door of the carpenter's shop. The pulpit, chancel rail, baptismal font, and other items of their creation preach as winsomely as could any pulpiteer.

A church in Knoxville, Tennessee, welcomed a retarded adult woman into membership. Another joined and the church started a Sunday school class. There proved to be a communication network of families having a retarded adult in their ranks. A harvest of retarded adults ensued, and many of their family members joined as well.

A church in Texas began a ministry to deaf people—complete with a sign language translator in the worship service. It attracted deaf people and their families—plus other people who wanted to join "a church that cares this much."

A church in Kenosha, Wisconsin, discovered more than a hundred first-generation Korean families living in Kenosha. They hired a Korean speaking lay pastor and started a growing Korean congregation within their church.

The possibilities of growth through relevant ministries for target populations are almost boundless for the congregation that can spot such populations and create special ministries for them. The price for such new ministries should be faced in advance, especially the additional staff time that such expanded outreach ministries will require.

9. *Reach people within the social network of your active Christians and new converts.* Donald McGavran's earliest research established that when the church is growing in certain Third World cultures, the faith spreads more naturally *within* a class, tribe, or caste than from one major social group to another. Indeed, cross-cultural outreach is more difficult and requires gifted and trained communicators. McGavran began counseling churches to especially witness along the lines of their social unit's social network. McGavran taught this as a paramount strategy for evangelism because the existing social network in a social unit will provide "The Bridges of God."[26] Non-Christians are much more receptive to credible Christian kinsmen or friends than to strangers or

even known members of other subcultures. Church growth inevitably *begins* by reaching cross-culturally into a previously unreached social unit and laboring to gain the first converts. Then, church growth *accelerates* as the new Christians reach out to their peers and other intimates within the social unit—and so "disciple it to the fringes."

For a while, we assumed that the "Bridges of God" strategy was more indigenous to Third World cultures than to countries like the U.S.A. But now research shows that the same principle takes its culturally appropriate forms in the West as well. For instance, Lyle Schaller has asked countless first generation members—"Why are you a member of this church?" Allowing some variation for region and culture, between two-thirds and three-fourths have given responses that can be classified as either *friendship ties* or *kinship ties.* Interestingly, members in stable or declining churches were most often won through kinship ties, while members of growing churches are most often won through friendship ties.[27] So, a strategic American church would continually work to locate and reach out to kinsmen, and especially to the friends of its active Christians and new converts. The church would also encourage its people to make new friends in the community continually. People are more receptive when they are approached by authentic Christians from within their social network.

10. *Reach out to persons in transition.* There is growing evidence that people who are experiencing (or have recently experienced) some major change in their life or social role are much more likely to be receptive to the gospel than during the periods of relative stability in their lives. We lack comprehensive data, but there are a number of such transitions that may help induce a period

of openness or responsiveness. Such transitions that most persons experience include: adolescence, going off to college or armed forces, first job, getting married, first child, last child leaving home ("empty nest syndrome"), menopause, male menopause, retirement, loss of a loved one, sickness. Additional receptivity-inducing transitions that many people experience include: moving to a new community, getting fired, job advancement, separation, divorce, second marriage. Notice, not all of these are experienced as crises. Nontraumatic transitions can still create receptivity. During and shortly after such transitions, people are likely to be very receptive to relevant ministries from a congregation. The congregation should be continually on the lookout for persons experiencing such transitions, in a diligent effort to perceive the good soil in which the Spirit is moving by his prevenient grace.

Of course, some of these transitions are likely to produce greater or longer receptivity than others. Ezra Earl Jones reminds us that the period of conception and birth of a first baby is a period that is also pregnant with religious possibilities. He instructs us that such receptive families now exist in unprecedented numbers!

For instance, the post-World War II baby boom lasted from 1945 until 1961. Those babies are now a special young adult generation—marrying later, starting families still later, having fewer children—but more families are having at least one child than ever before in American history. We are now in the early part of a fifteen to twenty year period during which there will be great numbers of young receptive families in the ministry areas of our churches. This should provide a great harvest of new disciples through the 1980s. Congregations which reach out to young families, with indigenous ministries to felt needs—starting new classes and groups for them, elevating them to visible leadership and enabling them to have a sense of ownership in the congregation's program and future—will grow!

A SUGGESTION FOR STRATEGY

What might all of this information look like as a congregation's grand strategy? It is one thing to state the principle: "reach out to undiscipled people in proportion to their relative receptivity." It is another thing to put that principle in action. One part of the strategy would be the congregation's classification of undiscipled people in the community. I suggest five classes:

1. receptive
2. interested
3. indifferent
4. resistant
5. hostile

The church might then visit:

1. receptive people every two weeks
2. interested people every four weeks
3. indifferent people every six weeks
4. resistant people every couple of months
5. hostile people every season

As people are perceived to change in their relative receptivity, reclassify them and visit accordingly.

We do not know nearly as much about receptivity as we want to. Available indicators and guidelines are not as precise as will one day be possible. But we have more to work with now than any previous generation has ever had. God has not abandoned our need for an adequate (if not perfect) strategy in this age of great missionary opportunity in the Western world. The church which takes seriously what we *do* know can experience unprecedented growth with apostolic power.

We do know that right now many people are receptive and searching, and we know from experience that the present opportunity for missionary expansion may not last indefinitely—at least, there are no guarantees. For this reason, McGavran exhorts the church to embrace its mission now.

Opportunity blazes today, but it may be a brief blaze. Certainly conditions which create the opportunity—as far as human wisdom can discern—are transient conditions. We have today. Let us move forward.[28]

CHAPTER VI

THE LOCAL CONGREGATION PUTS IT TOGETHER

A local church may enjoy growth for a while without sophisticated organizing and planning if something contagious is spontaneously occurring in its ministry or outreach. But effective year-by-year outreach and growth will take place only through a congregation organized for programmatic outreach.

It does matter how the evangelizing congregation is organized and deployed. The criteria for effectiveness include at least the following three: (1) All of the essential tasks in the total outreach enterprise must be defined. (2) The members must be matched, according to their perceived gifts, to the appropriate tasks. (3) The ministry of the organized evangelizing community must result in congregational growth from new disciples joining from the world. No organization or method should be retained which "ought to work," but does not. The means of evangelizing exist for the ends of helping people to become disciples of Jesus and find life in his body.

What follows is a demonstration of how this might be organized. It is assumed that the church takes seriously the fact that the ministry of witness is somewhat threatening to most lay people, that some Christian witnessers will have to learn to walk before they learn to run, and that although the various tasks in total outreach are not equally demanding, all the tasks are intrinsically worth doing and are part of the mission. I have arranged the tasks of organized outreach in increasing order of difficulty for the outreachers. Many of your people will find it possible now to do the easier tasks preparing some of them for the more rigorous tasks later. The tasks are also arranged acording to the several elements of the Great Commission found in Mt. 28:18-20, Mk. 16:15, Lk. 24:47-49, and Acts 1:8 and in the approximate order that the steps, principles, and experiences would take place.

"WAIT TO RECEIVE POWER"

Prior to launching out into the community, several things need to happen in the vision, structuring, and life of the congregation—especially within those members who will be part of the regular outreach ministry. I am not including two important elements in preparation—"analyzing the congregation's growth record" and "setting goals for new growth"—because they are now well covered in recent writings by Donald McGavran and Win Arn—*How To Grow a Church* and *Ten Steps to Church Growth*. Do include these elements in your preparation.

1. *Make a Discipleship Survey.* You need to begin a process of discovering the undiscipled people in your ministry area—i.e. people not presently following Jesus Christ through some community of faith. The discovery of a significant number of undiscipled people will help

your readers see the possibilities for growth and will build active interest in new programmatic outreach. You will discover prospects for discipleship by a door-to-door survey of your ministry area or selected target neighborhood.

Notice: You are not trying to discover people's "church preference." Seven out of ten people have a nominal church preference, or at least they think of something to say when being surveyed. Church preference surveys reap piles of data that are useless to you, unless you are especially interested in finding out the names of the churches people stay away from! The most useful data can be gathered by an indicator-question something like: "Are you currently attending any Christian congregation or group in this community?" Where a no is indicated, make sure the people's names and addresses are placed in your "Undiscipled Prospects File."

This surveying will give many of your people the experience that will free them for the more demanding tasks of outreach later on. But your central purpose in surveying is to record (on 3 x 5 index cards) the names and addresses of unchurched people (including nominal members not currently involved in any community of faith), and especially people who may be receptive.

2. *Begin Record Keeping.* The cards containing the data of prospective Christians should be filed, with one person in charge of the file. Because the cards represent people, the church should never risk losing a card. This is assured by giving outreach workers duplicate cards and *never* letting an original card leave the file. In time you will want to expand to two files—one based on the relative receptivity of persons (using the five categories: receptive, interested, indifferent, resistant, and hostile),

and one based on geographical sections of the ministry area, to enable the most visiting with the least traveling for your outreach teams.

3. *Begin Training for Outreach.* Your people will feel the need for some training and will be reluctant to reach out without it. The training ought to include: (a) scripture verses and principles of theology that inform evangelizing, including some consideration of the content of the message, (b) models of a local church engaged in evangelizing (such as Richard Armstrong's *The Oak Lane Story),* (c) and methods that can be employed by your people. Among the smorgasbord of methods available today, your choice ought to be guided by two criteria: the method you initially go with must be consistent with the theological tradition of your church, and it should continue to be used only if it is effective in communicating to your target population. This training period should also be characterized by (d) practice, which would include both role playing and on-the-job training (two trainees observing one experienced witnesser). Pervade all of this training with the emphasis that the most important task is the making of new friendships—which will then make evangelizing much more possible.

4. *Establish Evangelism Support Groups.* The ministry of witnessing is threatening work. All of your people will need the support of a group if they are to stick with and grow in the practice of evangelism. They should meet as a group immediately before going out, and immediately after. The understanding, learning, support, and empowerment that each person will receive from this *koinonia* is indispensible to the church's continued outreach.

5. *Pray for Empowerment.* Evangelism is primarily

The Local Congregation   133

the mission of the Holy Spirit, and only derivatively the mission of the church. The Spirit goes before us—creating receptivity in some people by his prevenient grace, and we follow him to those whom he has prepared. If what we say is perceived as the good news and the person responds to Jesus as Lord, this is happening because the Spirit is communicating to their being. And when we have appropriate words to say and the courage to reach out, this is because he is empowering us. We may know much about strategies and methods of communicating the gospel and evangelizing people but, whenever communication and response take place, it is his work communicated through our appropriate strategies and methods. We must always be more dependent on Christ's enabling Spirit than we are on even our best strategies and methods. This is so important that a group would be well advised to wait, perhaps for some weeks, until it had a sense of being visited, called, led out, and empowered by God's own presence.

"GO INTO YOUR WORLD"

Evangelistic strategy begins by achieving a presence and dialogue with the persons the church desires to attract into the Faith. Several tasks within this program for church evangelism stress our presence amidst the target population. Proclamation and persuasion may not be possible for now among resistant people. But achieving presence is intrinsically worthwhile, and may prepare people for proclamation, persuasion, and discipling. Of course, the witnesser who is trying to achieve presence should be open to attempting more when the person is receptive or when the Spirit leads. But in presence ministry, it is not necessary that one always (or even usually) verbalize the gospel; the Christian has not "failed Jesus" just because he has not mentioned his name. The essential purposes of presence ministry are to know people, to be known by them, to identify with them, and to demonstrate a caring interest in them, to build the friendships which can become the bridges of God. The following ministries of presence are important, and are less intimidating to new witnessers than are tasks which do mandate proclamation and/or disciplemaking.

6. *Telephone Ministries* are the least threatening form of "going," and some people have real gifts (and experience) for communicating over that medium. A variety of ministries can be performed over the telephone—from calls to people who have visited the church, to birthday and other special event calls, to crisis telepone ministries like *Contact.* Shut-in persons can frequently minister by telephone, especially to each other.

7. *Door-to-Door Friendly Visits* are manageable for many Christians. These visits go beyond surveying in that the purpose is to establish credibility, trust, and friendship and to discover needs to which the church can minister.

8. *Offering the Services of the Church to People* involves sharing a very particular facet of the good news to individuals and inviting response. Any church has (or should begin) ministries to meet the human needs that really are present in its ministry area. Day-care centers, mothers-day-out programs, meals-on-wheels, Parent Effectiveness Training, Big Brothers, counseling services, and special groups (scouts, senior citizens, etc.) are some random examples. Here the role of presence evangelism might be to inform people of these special services, inviting those who need them to participate. Or, the offer to serve might be more unstructured, as in the case of the

visitors from the Oak Lane Presbyterian Church in Philadelphia who ask people—"How can we be of help to you?"

9. *Visiting People Who Have Visited the Church's Worship Service* is a crucial presence ministry. People who visit your church are, statistically, among the most receptive people in your ministry area. They should be telephoned that afternoon and visited that week—and then somewhat regularly until their church involvement is decided, one way or another. The purpose of these visits is to express interest in people, to get to know them and be known by them, and to inquire regarding their beliefs, relation to Christ, and desires for Church membership. "Hard sell" to casual church visitors would be counter-productive. In this ministry you may very well engage in church referral. As you find out what people are looking for, if in your judgment another church could better meet their need—your greatest service might be to refer them to that church!

10. *Call on Inactive Members.* If inactive members were once worth winning, they are now worth reactivating. In certain cases, inactive members may be one of our most responsive populations because, as Canon Bryan Green reminds us, "They have something to return to." But if they are inactive because the church left them as new members outside the fellowship-involvement circle, they may be a quite resistant group. In any case, their renewal in the body of Christ requires the initiative of active church members. It is even worth talking to those whom we cannot reactivate—for the feedback they can give us. If we find out how we failed them, we may make the changes that will prevent us from failing others. Besides, for the sake of those who have not yet joined us, we need to love those who once

joined us. If we are perceived to shower attention on prospects while forgetting about members, then prospects understandably will be reluctant to join. "How those Christians love *one another*" is the ancient appeal which must be preserved. When prospects are loved, and they perceive that they will experience even more caring love within the community, they will desire to join that community.

"PREACH THE GOSPEL—
BE MY WITNESSES"

Some tasks within an evangelism program involve presence and also message-sharing. It is crucial that we share the gospel with all persons who "have the ears to hear" because "faith comes by hearing the word of God" and "it pleased God through the folly of what we preach to save those who believe." How is this witnessing to be done by today's Christian lay people? A rather elaborate answer will be found in the chapter "A New Model for Christian Witnessing," but some suggestions for relevant and effective forms of message-sharing are appropriate here. To maximize effectiveness, know in every congregation that the forms of witness used must be considered and indigenous. Slinging texts at people or regurgitating slogans before them will not be effective, nor can we blindly import methods that succeed in different populations. Our forms of witness must be creative and incarnational in ways that speak to secular people so that they can respond. The following forms represent some real possibilities that are available to many outreaching churches.

11. *Organize and Host Neighborhood Groups* in

which non-Christians can explore the Christian faith. The Church Growth Movement is discovering that many persons will come to a home meeting who would not come to a church building. But make sure that the non-Christians do not feel outnumbered. Have no more than two Christians present for every three non-Christians. The total number should not exceed fifteen. If it does, organize a second group. Such "outpost groups" should be considered top priority; organize as many as possible, because for many people they will be the threshold into the local church and Christian life. Their agenda must be the basics of the Christian gospel, expressed in quite secular language, correlating the message with the felt needs and motives of the receptive people who visit—and all of this within the setting of a warm, supportive, affirming fellowship. Occasionally non-Christians will volunteer their living rooms for such meetings; this is an opportunity that should be accepted.

12. *Christian Literature* is an often overlooked medium of proclaiming the gospel to non-Christians. Perhaps we overlook it because most people are turned off by tracts and because we think many people have stopped reading books. But in this generation the popularity of such books as *Love Story* and *Jonathan Livingston Seagull* teaches us that great numbers of people will read something interesting that can be completed in an evening. Discipleship Resources (the publishing arm of the United Methodist Board of Discipleship) reports great success in the sale of the "Pass-It-On" series, books such as: *How To Find God,* by Keith Miller; *Who Is Jesus Christ,* by William Barclay; and *What Is The Meaning of Life?* by Alan Walker.

Local churches could buy such books in quantity and give them to interested people. Individual witnessers who have mastered one of the books could then schedule a visit about the book after the person had a chance to read it. Or, a church might offer the books through a mass mailing to apartment dwellers, enclosing a return postcard for people to request that the book be delivered to them from the church. A witnesser would deliver the book to the apartment and stay only long enough to get acquainted, but would suggest that he/she stop back in two weeks at an appointed time to talk about the book. Any friends who had read it by then would also be welcome to join that conversation.

13. *Deploy Teams for Ministry and Witness to Persons in Transition.* There is abundant evidence that "people in transition are more receptive than people in stability." This principle applies to many transitions, and not merely the usual ones that are thought of as crises. The common transitions that most people experience, during (and shortly after) which they are likely to be more receptive include: adolescence, going to college or armed services, first job, getting married, first child, first child at an age to begin religious education, last child leaves home, menopause, male menopause, retirement. Common transitions that many people also experience include: moving, a suffering experience, loss of a loved one, separation, divorce, getting fired, job advancement. During and shortly after such changes in one's situation or social role, people tend to be fairly receptive to religious ministry and truth claims.

A church taking this fact with strategic seriousness would prepare cadres of its members for specific ministry and witness to persons in such transition. The gifts, interest, expertise, or background of a witnesser would be intentionally matched to a "transitional" ministry. For instance, a team of two or three Christians who had divorce in their background would be sent out to share the resources of grace and koinonia that they had discovered for this painful transition. Relevant Christian literature such as *Help! I've Been Fired,* by Clyde Reid, *The Will of God,* by Leslie Weatherhead and *Is There a Family in the House?* by Kenneth Chafin should be on hand in the church library for use in connection with these special ministries.

The church's strategy for persons in transition should be based on two elements. (a) Have a team of Christians for each transition, i.e., if you identify six transitions to which you can minister—have six teams. (b) Sensitize, by special effort, the entire congregation to their role as a referral system. For instance, if a church member hears of someone who was fired, is divorcing, or just retired, etc., that member would telephone the church secretary or other coordinator of this outreach program. The information would then be relayed to the appropriate ministry team of the church. This one comprehensive strategy can reach more people in periods of receptivity, and can use more Christians in accordance with their gifts, than any other single strategy with which I am familiar.

14. *Inviting Self-Actualizing People to Join in Service* is a neglected strategy in most churches, but it has great potential. Many persons may not currently have a sense of need which can be fulfilled by our offering of the gospel. Instead they may be motivated by the need for self-esteem or self-realization, a need which can be met as a by-product of giving themselves to some cause or service of the church's mission. If a church is doing worthwhile things for people, its most effective evangelical appeal to bright, strong, achievement-oriented persons will be to offer them the opportunity for

significant service through church projects and ministries to others. Through such experiences, many of these persons will "taste the Kingdom of God" and this experience will be self-authenticating. While participating in Christian service, longtime Christians will also be intentionally relating and witnessing to them. A fuller explanation of the gospel and causes of the faith will come out in appropriately natural conversation or in collaborative situations during the service experience as, for example, "Say, let me share with you more about why we Christians are engaged in this cause . . . "

15. *Door by Door Witnessing in a target neighborhood* is a genre which, although conventional, ought not be overlooked. It is not the most strategic way of deploying your witnessers; saturating receptive groups has a higher probability of harvest. But it is the only method of assuring that no person in your ministry area is neglected, and it is also an effective way of discovering receptive people.

Naturally, what you say to people, how, and where are crucial variables in this ministry. (See my "New Model for Christian Witnessing.") But we must take seriously our Lord's strong metaphor—"Do not cast your pearls before swine," i.e., we are not constrained to verbalize the gospel to persons now incapable of perceiving the gospel as great news. On some visits, only a ministry of presence and listening may be possible. We may appropriately ask permission to share something of our faith. And if people are in fact receptive, or at least open, we may indeed share a great deal. Our sharing should follow a careful listening to the other person so that we can correlate our witness to what we have perceived of the person's religious history and needs.

16. *Visit the Town Agnostics and the "Tough Situations."* We are not called to abandon any people or setting. Some of our more articulate and inwardly strong Christians should visit bars, jails, City Hall, or whatever settings and peoples are indifferent or hostile to Christ and the church. The direct returns from such ministry will be fairly low, but it will strengthen witnessers engaged in this apologetic ministry, and it will establish the public image of the church as a community that both cares and dares.

17. *"Make Disciples."* Everything that we do in the preparation, presence, and proclamation ministries is for the sake of making disciples, i.e., persuading people to become followers of Jesus through his Body the church. None of the strategies in this chapter so far are ends in themselves—although many are intrinsically worth doing.

God calls to people in Jesus Christ that they might turn to him—open their beings to him—obey him—become members of his body—and so find life. For this reason the ministry of "discipling" requires that at some time we share the gospel and appeal for response. That "time" is God's *Kairos* or moment when a person is perceived as being receptive or when the course of an evangelical conversation naturally leads to that point. This is the most awesome task in a church's program of outreach, but it is indispensable. Some of your people will have the spiritual gifts to lead people, not only toward, but into an initial Christian experience. All witnessers should extend the option when they find an opportunity, but your lay "discipling specialists" should be sent to persons who are thought to be on the threshold of a decision to commit their life to Christ.

"BAPTIZE THEM INTO THE
CHURCH AND TEACH THEM"

Bishop J. Waskom Pickett demonstrated four decades ago that what we do with people in the weeks immediately after they join the church is crucial. Indeed, his study of about four thousand converts in India concluded that their postbaptismal training was more influential in whether they remained and grew in the Christian community than even the motives which originally attracted them to Christianity. I am sure that the first few weeks are equally important to the life of a new convert in any American church.

18. *Membership Training* is a very important element in the new convert's incorporation into Christ's church. No convert ought to be "spared" this instruction which should be very basic in content: Ten Commandments, Lord's Prayer, Apostles Creed; general introduction to the Bible plus concentration on one or two books—say Luke and Galatians; and an introduction to the church and the mission of Christian lay people. A text, such as Michael Green's *New Life, New Lifestyle,* might be used. Church Growth literature teaches that such training might best begin immediately after a person's decision to follow Jesus and join the church—whenever these occur—and not at some predetermined age or prior to joining. Also, such training might best be done on a one-to-one tutoring basis in the convert's house—with the convert's family welcome to join in the lessons.

19. *The Relational Support System.* The convert's solid entry into the church is not merely the cognitive entry which membership training enables, but also a relational entry. The church must move intentionally to build a relational support system that will create in the

convert a sense of being known and belonging to the people of God. New members not brought into a circle of fellowship are soon lost to inactivity. Two strategies are especially promising.

One strategy is a *sponsors program*. The convert is assigned a sponsor (or in the case of a couple, a sponsoring couple). A sponsor ought to represent the same homogeneous population as the convert. The sponsor will introduce the new member to people, groups, and opportunities in the church. The sponsor will be available to the new member, will occasionally ask him how things are going, and will probably visit him monthly at some length for the first year of the new member's life in the congregation. The original "matchup" between sponsor and convert is not etched in granite. If it turns out that they are "mismatched," the convert should be assigned another sponsor. Fairly recent converts (one to four years) frequently make excellent sponsors, so look among your growing converts for promising sponsors. The pastor should have a quarterly support and instruction meeting for sponsors.

The other basic strategy for relational support is your church's *group system*. Every convert ought to become quickly involved in the life of some group connected with your church, whether a Sunday school class, a prayer group, an action group, a choir, or an age group. Group involvement ought to be required for the converts (as for all members), because most Christians cannot remain vital or grow in life except as that Life is mediated through Christian koinonia. But not all persons will want small group experiences; large group involvements should be offered as options.

20. *Opportunities for Acting in Discipleship.* The new convert's entry into Christian life and community is not

only cognitive and relational, but also behavioral. The Christian possibility becomes incarnate in the personality of the believer as a by-product of obedient Christian behavior. This implies two additional requirements. One is frequent corporate worship, in which the convert rehearses and reinforces his newly chosen identity within the identity and story of the people of God. The other requirement is service. Every convert is called to engage in whatever roles or tasks of the church are appropriate to the gifts within the individual—as perceived by the body and its leaders. This too is crucial in the assimilation of new members—without which we tend to lose them to inactivity.

Conversion and maturation in the faith are cognitive and relational and behavioral. Therefore, just as we said that evangelism takes place through kerygma, koinonia, and diakonia, so, many Christians say that actual incorporation into the body and maturation in the faith take place through those same three resources plus *leitourgia* (worship). Together, these four resources of the Christian church can engage the person in the totality of his/her personality and motivation structure. But if the church withholds even one of these four resources from a person, then there is a part of that person not engaged with the gospel, and the chances of retarded spiritual growth or of losing the person after a time are immeasurably greater.

THE CONTAGIOUS CONGREGATION'S
MISSION BEYOND THE PARISH

I once saw a painting of a "dead church" in a magazine. The sanctuary was exquisite and inspiring, it was full of people wearing their "Sunday best," the pastor was robed and cultured—but in one corner cobwebs covered over the coin slot in a box marked "missions." That picture dramatizes a frequent cause of a congregation's lack of contagion—they live for themselves. At the opposite extreme of John Wesley's declaration that "The world is my parish," the noncontagious congregation says "Our parish is our world." Practically speaking, Wesley's challenge reaches out beyond our parish and points us to the bold reembracing of three areas of the church's larger mission.

One area of the congregation's wider evangelistic concern will be aggressive support for the "planting" of many new congregations. Your goal in evangelization is to reach out and make disciples. But there are many people in your city or county who are geographically or culturally beyond the reach of your congregation. They live too far away, or you don't speak their language, or your ministries do not engage their felt needs. Your congregation cannot reach them in significant numbers, but a new church strategically planted—near them and for them and culturally indigenous to them—could reap a harvest. Ignore the faddists who complain that church extension is "not where it's at," the mothering of daughter churches is a necessary component in faithfulness to the Great Commission. Ignore those who complain that new churches "cost too much;" new congregations represent your denomination's greatest potential investment.

Strategically placed, new congregations grow. A recent study of Presbyterian membership trends shows that while the United Presbyterian Church in the U.S.A. has been declining at a rate of 1.9 percent per year, their first generation congregations have been growing at a rate of 9.8 percent per year. Note also that growing denominations are planting new congregations in very great numbers—even in the political units where they already have a church—as in the case of Southern Baptists who started new congregations in Texas at a rate of 138 in 1975, 189 in 1976, and 400 for 1977–78! Likewise, as Dr. Kenneth Chatin declares, "Show me a denomination that is not aggressively starting new congregations, and I'll show you a denomination that is already in the terminal condition!"

The second area of wider opportunity is your congregation's strong support of global missions and evangelization. There are almost three billion unreached people on our planet. And four-fifths of these people have no Christians in their social unit who can share the possibility with them. They can only be reached, and evangelical movement can only begin among them, when we support and send out great numbers of cross-cultural missionaries to "make disciples among the peoples." Fortunately, many of the world's peoples are now very receptive—mandating extensive outreach "while the fields are ripe unto harvest."

Strongly supporting church extension and world missions would not "cost" your congregation a thing. Indeed, the congregation would grow as a by-product, because many people are more likely to join a church that is in mission beyond its parish. Missionary involvement especially adds to a congregation's magnetism when it not only supports missions, but also deploys lay people in cross-cultural outreach. The Southern Baptists of Texas are commissioning a thousand lay people to help start a thousand congregations in Brazil in 1983. Their Texas congregations will grow as a by-product.

We in United Methodism have discovered this indirect "payoff" from the missionary involvement of lay people—especially in cases where laity experience all three resources of the gospel. A program called the Appalachian Service Project has demonstrated this as significantly as anything I know. Its leader, the late Tex Evans, a longtime missionary to Appalachian people, began taking church members—especially youth—into Appalachia to work with Appalachian people on their homes—painting, digging wells, building porches—and relating to them in Christian friendship and witness.

The pattern began in 1970. Today, a group moves in for a week, living at Union College. During the day they work with Appalachian people on their houses, relating to them and accepting them just as they are. In the evening the visiting groups establish a worshiping fellowship—sharing, singing, praying, celebrating, cheering. They study the Scriptures which inform their ministry, learning how with Christ they can open doors to captives and share good news with the poor, discovering that as they do this unto one of the least of Christ's brothers, they do this unto him.

This Appalachian Service Project has tapped a wellspring of national response. We now know that great numbers of people are eager to serve—and if the church will create an opportunity for them to serve in a significant way with Christ it will make a difference in people's lives—they will serve, they will become renewed, and their home churches will experience renewal and greater contagion. Below, the snow-balling track record of the Appalachian project shows the increasing number of people who became involved in it, and the work they did.

Year	People	Houses
1970	387	50
1971	658	110
1972	1033	131
1973	1612	236
1974	2735	418

By design, the numbers have now leveled off to about 4000–5000 participants each summer, working with 500-600 homes and families.

One summer, Kathy Williams, a lovely sixteen-year-old girl from the United Methodist Church of Seaford, Delaware, was singing a song that she had written as she reflected upon her experiences in Appalachia. They asked her to sing the song for Tex, and he was so thrilled by it that the song has found its way into the legends of the Appalachia Service Project. The words of the song do not render aesthetically perfect poetry, but they do illustrate the love, the change, and the new Christian identification that comes as a by-product of fellowship, message, and service.

Chorus: Our hearts are in the hills
Where the rain comes
pouring down.
The Lord of Love will help
us through
And we'll tell of the love we
have found.

First Verse: Way down in the bottom of
a holler
We found some folk with
their walls
all tumbling down

We helped them that
morning with our faith in
  God
And we made those dear
walls become strong

Second Verse: They smiled so big and
wide,
And through the rain we
saw the sun
With a brand new porch on
the front of their house
That they had never seen
before.

Third Verse: Goodbye, we said as we
walked away
With the tears all flowing
down
The God of Love will help
us through
And we'll tell of the love we
have found.

As *your* lay people support and become involved in
the mission beyond the parish, your mission to your
parish will grow in clarity, power, and effectiveness.

AND FINALLY

Supremely, the contagious congregation is magnetic
for receptive people because it sees and is gripped and
driven by a vision of what is possible for people and the
world if the gospel is only shared. I have tried for years to

adequately express this vision, and its power upon me, but am not yet confident that I have semantically corraled the vision of the Great Commission. Another generation set it to poetry better than has ours, so let me leave you with the apostolic expressions of Blake (slightly modified) and Lindsey:

I shall not cease from mental strife,
nor shall the sword slip from my hand—
Until we have built Jerusalem
in America's green and searching land.

This is our faith tremendous—
Our wild hope, and who shall scorn?
That in the name of Jesus
The world shall be reborn.

NOTES

CHAPTER I

1. Lyle E. Schaller and Charles A. Tidwell, *Creative Church Administration* (Nashville: Abingdon, 1975), pp. 150–53.

2. See such books by Colin Williams as *Where In The World* (New York: National Council of Churches, 1963), *What In The World* (New York: National Council of Churches, 1964), and Faith in a Secular *Age* (New York: Harper, 1966).

3. C. Peter Wagner, *Frontiers in Missionary Strategy* (Chicago: Moody Press, 1971). I am indebted to Dr. Wagner for the stimulus which resulted in these five categories. Wagner employs three categories—presence, proclamation, and persuasion. I have deviated from Wagner for two reasons. (1) His "proclamation" category mixes apples and oranges; i.e., it includes both the appeal to "Hear the Word" and the appeal to "Make a Decision." At least in American culture, those two approaches are different enough to warrant separate categories. (2) I have refrained from using the label "persuasion" for any one type because, as I have described them, *each* of the five ministries employs persuasion.

4. D. T. Niles, *That They May Have Life* (New York: Harper, 1951) pp. 82–83.

5. Think, for instance, of that chap who can tell you about the time he "gave his heart to Jesus," but who today, years later, is not a biblically-informed Christian, his church membership is nominal, his involvement in service and mission is "invisible" at best. Or, think of the woman who "has read the Bible from Genesis to Revelation five times," but is not a disciple of Jesus, nor found in Jesus' special family, nor is she known by her neighbors to be a person who loves and serves—her religious knowledge notwithstanding. Or, think of the fellow who is "a charter member of this congregation" and is found present "religiously" in the same pew fifty-two Sundays per year—but still doesn't understand elementary Christianity, is not involved in any service or mission appropriate to his gifts, and, indeed, has used his locked-in "Churchianity" as a way to evade any meeting with Jesus Christ. Or think of the woman in your community who does good deeds and supports the right causes—but her good activity is not normed and informed by the gospel's revelation of God's will for his children in community, she is not consciously "in Christ," her frequent compassion-fatigue clobbers her because she lacks the support and renewing power of Christian koinonia, and so she flits from one cause, to another, and another, without seeing any of them through. Or she sticks with one cause, but not knowing she is already justified by grace, she spends decades using that cause to justify her own existence rather than living for the cause.

6. I am aware of the challenge by Donald McGavran to the kerygma, koinonia, diakonia formula, in 1965. At that time, he saw it as a fashionable "sacred triad" of activities being indulged in as ends in themselves, and therefore, were "in danger of subordinating the spread of the gospel" to these activities. See his article, "Wrong Strategy—The Real Crisis in Mission," now reprinted in *The Conciliar-Evangelical Debate: The Crucial Documents 1964–1976* (South Pasadena, California: William Carey Library, 1977) p. 101. I very much hope that my own delineation of these resources and their use has overcome such objections, because I believe that the earliest supporters of the formula were vulnerable to McGavran's charges. I have developed the triad's rationale very differently from J. C. Hoekendijk and earlier writers, showing its relevance to the structure of human motivation, and its usefulness in arranging the resources of the gospel—with the dominant intention of *enhancing the spread of the gospel.*

CHAPTER II

1. Kenneth Scott Latourette, *A History of the Expansion of Christianity,* Vol. 1 (Grand Rapids: Zondervan, [1937], 1973), chapter 4.

2. Keith Miller, *The Becomers* (Waco, Tex.: Word Books, 1973).

3. See Abraham H. Maslow, *Motivation and Personality,* (New York: Harper, 1970), chapter 3 and chapter 4. Maslow's content is eclectic, derived from the insights of several schools of psychology. But the hierarchy structuring is his enduring contribution, and its content was confirmed in Maslow's own research.

4. *Ibid,* p. 46.

5. *Ibid.,* p. 51.

6. The heart of Bonhoeffer's contentions about man having "come of age" and the consequent need for a "religionless Christianity" can be found in his *Letters and Papers From Prison* (New York: MacMillan, 1953), pp. 162–69, 219–20, 225–26.

7. An excellent case study of a declining congregation in a transitional urban neighborhood that "turned it around," became contagious, and experienced significant growth. See Richard S. Armstrong, *The Oak Lane Story,* (New York: Div. of Evangelism, Board of National Missions, United Presbyterian Church in the U.S.A., 1971). Key excerpts can be found in Tetsunao Yamamori and E. Leroy Lawson, *Church Growth: Everybody's Business* (Cincinnati: Standard Publishing, 1975), pp. 127–29.

8. Samuel Southard, *Pastoral Evangelism* (Nashville: Broadman Press, 1962), pp. 43-47.

9. For the near-current state of research on this important theme, see Joe M. Bohlen, "Research Needed on Adoption Models," in Wilbur Schramm and Donald F. Roberts, eds., *The Process and Effects of Mass Communication,* (Urbana: University of Illinois Press, 1972), pp. 798–815.

10. This material is adapted from Bryan Green, *The Practice of Evangelism* (New York: Scribner's, 1951), chap. 6, pp. 139–64. All quotations in this section are from this chapter by Canon Green—which may be the best material yet written on this subject in evangelism literature.

CHAPTER III

1. See especially Aristotle's *The Rhetoric of Aristotle,* L. Cooper, ed. (New York: Appleton-Century Crofts, 1932).

2. This is the thesis of the famous first lecture of Finney's *Lectures* on *Revivals of Religion.* The best study edition is the one edited by William G. McLaughlin (Cambridge: Harvard University Press, 1960).

3. Perhaps the best contemporary explication of Aristotle's model is Edward P. J. Corbett's *Classical Rhetoric for the Modern Student* (New York: Oxford University Press, 1971).

4. There are a number of published examples of Soper's style of "beginning where people are." They include *Christ and Tower Hill* (London: Hodder and Stoughton, 1934), *Question Time on Tower Hill* (London: Hodder and Stoughton, 1935), *Answer Time on Tower Hill* (London: Hodder and Stoughton, 1936), and *Christianity and Its Critics* (London: Hodder and Stoughton, 1937). The most recent and representative is *Tower Hill,* 12:30 (London: Epworth Press, 1963).

5. See the new edition of Campbell's *The Philosophy of Rhetoric* edited by Lloyd F. Bitzer, (Carbondale: Southern Illinois University Press, 1963), pp. 77. Chapters 1 and 7 contain Campbell's full delineation of his understanding of the communicator's appeal to the passions.

6. *Ibid.,* p. 78.

7. This is Minnick's thesis developed in chapter 9 of his *The Art of Persuasion,* 2d ed. (Boston: Houghton Mifflin, 1968), pp. 232–51. His chapter 8 contains an excellent discussion of motivation theory for the would-be advocate.

8. Thonssen, Baird, and Braden, *Speech Criticism,* 2d ed. (New York: Ronald Press, 1970), p. 430.

9. William Warren Sweet, *Revivalism in America* (Nashville: Abingdon Press, 1944), p. xii.

10. Modern experimental studies have isolated several factors in addition to Aristotle's—such as credibility and dynamism. For a useful survey of modern research on this subject, see Kenneth E. Anderson and Theodore Clevenger, Jr., "A Summary of Experimental Research in Ethos," *Speech Monographs,* 30, (June, 1963), 59–78.

11. See Kenneth Burke, *A Rhetoric of Motives* (Berkeley: University of California Press, 1969), pp. 19–23, 55–59.

12. Helmut Thielicke, *The Trouble With the Church* (New York: Harper, 1965), pp. 3–11.

13. These are the two major theses of Dean Kelley's somewhat controversial book, *Why Conservative Churches are Growing,* rev. ed. (New York: Harper, 1977).

14. As quoted in Thonssen, Baird, and Braden, *Speech Criticism,* p. 445.

CHAPTER IV

1. This perennial waiting by churchmen for the "perfect method," which, like a stretch sock, is easily grasped and will fit any situation, is (hopefully) one of the few remnants of primitive magic that remains in Protestant personalities. I call it "magic" in the quite literal and classical sense—the primitive assumption that if you learn the right words to say and you say them right, then you receive the supernatural results that you purposed.

In evangelism, reliance upon the rehearsed, learned, repeated incantation is still with us. Such a dependency upon a "magic method" is usually ineffective because it violates two important principles: (1) No one method can reach all people. In a given missionary setting, one's method must be indigenous to the culture of the target population. (2) People who are presently very resistant probably cannot be won by any evangelistic method, for now, because resistance is real—and is not the simple illusion many evangelicals assume it to be.

2. Donald A. McGavran, *Understanding Church Growth* (Grand Rapids: Eerdmans, 1970) chap. 12.

3. *Ibid.,* pp. 229–30.

4. *Ibid.,* pp. 230–31.

5. Although this is my own form of the definition, all of its elements are found in the work of such writers as Charles West, Richard Schaull, and Harvey Cox. See epecially Cox's *The Secular City* (New York: MacMillan, 1965).

6. This thesis is developed in Tawney's *Religion and the Rise of Capitalism* (Harmondsworth, Middlesex, England: Penguin Books, 1922).

7. This is the thesis of Martin E. Marty's splendid study, The *Modern Schism: Three Paths to the Secular* (London; SCM Press, 1969).

8. Kelley, *Conservative Churches,* see especially chap. 3, "The Indispensable Function of Religion."

9. Donald O. Soper, *The Advocacy of the Gospel* (Nashville: Abingdon, 1961). The first chapter has been reprinted in George G. Hunter, ed., *Rethinking Evangelism,* (Nashville: Tidings, 1971). The best collection of Soper's actual advocacy to resistant secular people is in his book, *Tower Hill, 12:30.*

10. See G. M. Trevelyan, *Illustrated English Social History,* Vol. 2

(Harmondsworth, Middlesex: England, Penguin Books, 1964), p. 100.

11. As quoted in Soper, *The Advocacy,* p. 18.

12. *Ibid.,* p. 19. Soper believes that this change to widespread doubt contributes to resistance within the evangelist's receptors. "Consequently, before we can make any impression upon those to whom we seek to preach today, we have to recognize that they are already in a resistant frame of mind. They have been encouraged to think very largely in terms of doubt, and the more authoritatively we claim to speak, the more likely we are to produce an ambivalent, if not a contrary, effect to that which we desire. This is the outstanding characteristic of the hearer."

13. Donald O. Soper, "Donald Soper on Preaching to Doubters," *The Methodist Recorder,* (May 24, 1962).

14. Much of this material is from Soper's remarks to a 1971 Conference on Cooperative Evangelism, published as "What I Have Learned About Communicating With the Outsider" in Harold Bales, ed., *Bridges to the World* (Nashville: Tidings, 1971), pp. 42–54.

15. *Ibid.,* p. 47.

16. The best source showing Soper's stress on teaching the faith to the public is the last chapter of his *Popular Fallacies About the Christian Faith* (London: Epworth Press, 1938, Wyvern Books, [1957]).

17. Stephen Neill, "Conversion," *The Scottish Journal of Theology,* 8, 1951.

18. See Kelly, *Why Conservative Churches,* pp. 49–51 and 99–102.

19. Donald O. Soper, "Challenge to the Church," *The Daily Herald* (London), 11 January 1937.

20. Soper, *Tower Hill, 12:30,* p. 136.

CHAPTER V

1. See McGavran, *Understanding,* chap. 12 and Wagner, *Frontiers,* chap. 6.

2. From Arthur F. Glasser, "An Introduction to the Church Growth Perspectives of Donald Anderson McGavran," in *Theological Perspectives on Church Growth,* ed., Harvie M. Conn (The Den Dulk Foundation, 1976), p. 38.

3. McGavran, *Understanding,* pp. 216, 218.

5. *Ibid.,* p. 230.

5. See Donald A. McGavran and Winfield C. Arn, *Ten Steps for Church Growth,* (New York: Harper, 1977), chap. 6. There is also much suggestive and helpful material in McGavran and Arn's earlier collaboration—*How To Grow A Church,* (Glendale, California: B/L Publications, 1973), chap. 3.

6. McGavran and Arn, *Ten Steps,* p. 76.

7. Wagner, *Frontiers,* p. 121.

8. McGavran and Arn, *Ten Steps,* p. 76.

9. McGavran's concept of the "Homogenous Unit" (discussed later in this chapter) is the most controversial of the Church Growth school's teachings. It is simply McGavran's shorthand term for the consciousness of "class" or "kind" that in fact characterizes a great many people in most, if not all, societies. McGavran observed that the faith spreads more naturally and with fewer obstacles *within* a given population unit than if people are invited to become disciples by joining a church composed primarily of people of a different population unit. The homogeneous unit principle is related to the strategy of making outreach indigenous to the people of a particular culture or subculture.

10. McGavran, *Understanding,* p. 229.

11. From Roy E. Shearer, "The Psychology of Receptivity and Church Growth," in *God, Man, and Church Growth,* ed., A. R. Tippett (Grand Rapids: Eerdmans, 1973), p. 162.

12. Edward C. Pentecost, *Reaching the Unreached* (South Pasadena, Calif.: William Carey Library, 1974), pp. 98–99.

13. Wagner, *Frontiers,* p. 113.

14. This is explained in an article now classic in cultural anthropology by Anthony F. C. Wallace, "Revitalization Movements," *American Anthropologist,* (April, 1956), 269. This same basic understanding of the kind of human psychological condition that makes attitude change or new commitment possible has been identified by a number of scholars in several different fields. Perhaps the most useful theories yet articulated are the "Balance Model" of Abelson and Rosenbert, the "Congruity" principle of Osgood and Tannenbaum, and especially the "Cognitive Dissonance Theory" of Leon Festinger. These theories are thoroughly explained in Roger Brown, *Social Psychology* (New York: The Free Press, 1965), chap. 11. Suggestions for their use by the advocate can be found in Wayne N. Thompson, *The Process of Persuasion* (New York: Harper, 1975), chap. 8.

15. This is McGavran's thesis in *Understanding,* chap. 13.

16. Shearer, "Receptivity and Church Growth," pp. 162–63.

17. McGavran, *Understanding,* p. 219.

18. Wagner, *Frontiers,* p. 112.

19. McGavran, *Understnding,* p. 220.

20. Wagner, *Frontiers,* p. 114.

21. *Ibid.*

22. *Ibid.,* p. 112.

23. McGavran, *Understanding,* p. 223.

24. See Paul G. Hiebert, *Cultural Anthropology* (Philadelphia: Lippencott, 1976), chap. 9 and chap. 14.

25. This is one of the seven characteristics that Schaller has discovered in virtually all growing American Protestant congregations that he has researched. See Schaller and Tidwell, *Creative Church Administration,* pp. 150–53.

26. This was the thesis developed in McGavran's original bombshell, *The Bridges of God* (United Kingdom: World Dominion Press, 1955).

27. See Lyle E. Schaller, "Six Targets for Growth," *The Lutheran* (September 3, 1975).

28. Donald A. McGavran, *How Churches Grow* (New York: Friendship Press, 1959), p. 9.

The Contagious Congregation